DAILY DRUM WARM-UPS

by Andy Ziker

D0504051

Contents

To access audio visit:
www.halleonard.com/mylibrary

Enter Code
6276-5888-0505-6041

ISBN: 978-1-4234-9518-5

HAL•LEONARD®
7777 W. BLUEMOUND RD. P.O. BOX 13819 MILWAUKEE, WI 53213

Audio Track Listing

Drums by Andy Ziker.
Produced by Andy Ziker and Tim Downs and engineered by Tim Downs at Winston Recording.

INTRODUCTION

WHY WARM UP BEFORE DRUMMING?

British scientists have recently demonstrated that drumming can be quite an intense workout. "Live rock drumming performance relies heavily upon the interplay between aerobic and anaerobic energy systems," researcher Marcus Smith from Chichester University explained in a 2008 study. Using Blondie drummer Clem Burke as a test subject, Smith revealed that 90 minutes of drumming can raise your heart rate to as high as 190 beats per minute and burn 400–600 calories per hour.

Drumming can be just as demanding as basketball, tennis, soccer, and many other sports. Players in these sports routinely warm up as part of a pre-game ritual to prevent injury and increase endurance. It follows that drummers should include warming up as part of a regular regimen.

Some of the benefits of warming up before drumming include:

- Increased range of motion and decreased risk of injury related to repetition, such as tennis elbow, shoulder tendonitis, carpal tunnel syndrome, and various strains and sprains.

- Increased heart rate and circulation. While playing exercises from *Daily Drum Warm-Ups*, you will actually feel a tingling sensation associated with raised blood flow. This helps deliver oxygen to the muscles involved and provides greater strength and stamina.

- Decreased muscle tension. Your body temperature goes up while warming up, increasing your muscle's elasticity.

- Focused mind. Warming up increases concentration and mentally prepares you for practicing or performing.

- Skill/technique development. Drumming can involve loud, fast, and technically-challenging passages. It's easy to tense up during these moments, raising the chance of injury. Practicing technical exercises trains the body (and mind) to relax during strenuous bursts.

As you make warm-ups part of your daily routine, you'll also notice gradual improvement in your playing. For instance, by warming up using paradiddles, it will become easier to apply this rudiment to the drumset.

WAYS TO WARM UP

You can prepare to play the drums in a number of ways:

- Take a hot shower. It may seem strange to take a hot shower and then proceed to sweat while drumming. Nevertheless, hot water therapy is a proven way to warm up.

    NOTE: *This is not a recommended method in drought-ravaged locales.*

- Move to a warm climate. I notice that when it is over 100 degrees in Phoenix, I don't need to warm up very much. When it is 120 degrees, I don't need to warm up at all!

- Stretch or follow a yoga routine. My book, *Drum Aerobics* (Hal Leonard Corporation, HL06620137), details a stretching routine designed specifically for drummers.

- Dance. Tai Chi is a Chinese form of martial arts that warms up both the mind and body in a relaxed, methodical manner.

    NOTE: *You could substitute other forms of dance, such as tap, hip-hop, or jazz into your warm-up, though you might receive some strange looks from fellow musicians.*

- Go for a brief aerobic workout: Get on an exercise bike, an elliptical trainer, or a treadmill, or take a walk, a jog, or jump rope. Because in this case these activities are used as warm-ups, do them for no more than three to five minutes.

- Practice meditation. This is a valuable discipline that relaxes both the body and mind.

- Use *Daily Drum Warm-Ups*. Right/left hand (stick) exercises warm up the upper body. Combined with foot ostinatos, the exercises will stimulate greater blood flow to the entire body.

ESSENTIAL SKILLS

You will realize immediate results in your playing if you do the warm-ups from this book on a daily basis. There are 12 types of exercises included in *Daily Drum Warm-Ups* to maximize your development as a drummer:

1. **Rudiments, Hybrid Rudiments, and Simple Patterns:** In many circles (including some drum circles), rudiments are considered to be the building blocks of drumming. This is for good reason: They require an understanding of sticking (whether you use a right or left stick), accents, rhythm, and the technique of efficient motion. Rudiments are combinations of single strokes, double strokes, flams, and drags combined into short musical phrases.

- **Single strokes** occur when the sticks play an alternating pattern (RLRL or LRLR) with each stick bouncing one time off the drumhead.

- **Double strokes** (RRLL or LLRR) arise when one wrist motion (followed by subsequent wrist motions) causes the stick to bounce twice off the head in a controlled manner.

The fingertips extend out (but still make contact with the stick) at the end of the downstroke and control the stick after the second rebound.

- The music notation symbol for a **flam** is ♪♩. The small note is normally a grace note (a soft hit), while the larger note is often played as an accent. In a traditional flam, the grace note strikes right before the primary note, creating a thicker sound.

- The music notation symbol for a **drag** (often called a ruff) is ♫♪. A drag is very much like a flam, except that two grace notes are played right before a primary note.

In both the case of the flam and the drag, a grace note starts out about 2 inches from the drumhead and the regular note starts out at about 12 inches. The grace note is a tap or an upstroke while the regular note is a downstroke.

NOTE: Many of the rudiments in Daily Drum Warm-Ups *are engraved in a more practical style (to make them easier to read and to apply to the drumset) than the more time-honored, traditional manner.*

- **Hybrid rudiments**, which can be defined as rudiments outside the spectrum but related to the "essential 13," the "original 26" from the National Association of Rudimental Drummers (NARD), or the 40 Essential Rudiments (the Percussive Arts Society, PAS, added 14 more), are used in *Daily Drum Warm-Ups*. Hybrids are typically combinations of the 40 Essential Rudiments, such as flams merged with double-strokes.

- Short musical phrases, called **Simple Patterns**, are also included in the book. These fit beyond the realm of rudiments or hybrid rudiments, but are, nevertheless, integral to drumset playing.

2. **Accent Patterns:** Accent patterns in *Daily Drum Warm-Ups* include single strokes, double strokes, paradiddles, and double paradiddles played as 16th notes, eighth-note triplets, swung eighth notes, and sextuplets.

Accents are produced by first bending your arm at your elbow (as if you were doing a reverse bicep curl), so that the tip of the stick points up toward the sky. Because the stick is now higher off the playing surface, it needs to come down with more force to make up the distance. This produces a stroke that sounds louder than the unaccented notes.

Try not to produce accents in an inefficient way with the wrists only. (See photo on the left.) Instead, use the shoulder, elbow, wrist, and fingers to accomplish the accent. (See photo on the right.)

Stroke/Tap Instructions can be used to help break down Accent Patterns into their component parts. This will allow better understanding of the playing motion, freeing you up to play with greater speed and efficiency. Visit another one of my books, *Drumcraft* (published by Cherry Lane), for detailed descriptions and a clear pictorial of how this system works.

NOTE: *The music notation symbol for accents is* >, *known in mathematics as a "greater than" sign.*

One way of producing accents is by playing rim shots. Rim shots produce a cutting, high-frequency sound.

A rim shot is generated when the middle portion of the stick hits the rim of the drum at the same time as the tip of the stick hits near the center of the drum.

3. **Moeller:** The Moeller Technique is a study in efficient motion, allowing you to play with speed, endurance, finesse, and power. It involves the use of a whipping motion when performing down strokes or full strokes (accented notes) and the fingers/wrist when executing taps or upstrokes (unaccented notes).

The following photo sequence shows Moeller 3s, which consist of a downstroke, followed by a tap, and then an upstroke.

Notice the stick pointing upward (the position of the stick during the whipping motion, when the stick is about to fly downward). Also, notice the change of angle of the stick during the next two unaccented hits (the tap and the upstroke).

NOTE: *Stroke/Tap Instructions can also be used to break down the component movements of the Moeller exercises. Again, take a look at* Drumcraft *for a complete description of this technique.*

4. **Weak Hand Builders:** These exercises are designed for the right-handed drummer who wants to improve their left hand. Left-handed drummers should reverse the stickings so their weak hand is receiving the greatest workout.

5. **Rhythm Builders:** Sight-reading exercises are offered here in gradually increasing levels of difficulty. Because you will be both reading and playing these, Rhythm Builders are both a physical and mental warm-up.

For more practice with building your sense of rhythm, *Drumcraft* details a novel, foolproof method for reading, writing, and playing rhythms using the concept of subdividing. It also ventures into methods for making logical sticking choices, which often makes reading and playing rhythms easier.

For additional help in reading/playing the rhythms found in the book, you can use the 4/4 Time Chart and the Example/Audio Track as a point of reference.

6. **Rudimental Recipes:** These warm-ups combine rudiments and hybrid rudiments to make interesting musical mishmashes. When applied to the drumset, these recipes will add plenty of flavor to your drumming.

Reading combinations of rudiments can be difficult. If you strip away the accents, flams, ruffs, and double strokes, a rhythmic skeleton is left behind. This is a good place to start.

7. **Combos:** These warm-ups combine rudiments, hybrid rudiments, simple patterns, accent patterns, Moeller, rhythm builders, BZZzz's, and triple strokes all in one!

8. **BZZzz's:** BZZzz strokes are also known as multiple bounce or press rolls and are accomplished by tightening the fulcrum between the first three fingers (thumb, pointer, and middle finger) and pressing the tip of the stick into the playing surface. You will notice that each stick will produce approximately 12 bounces. When played in an alternating fashion (RLRL), the multiple bounces overlap, producing a smooth or legato roll.

Because BZZzz's involve multiple bounces per hand, fast wrist pulsations are normally not required.

9. **Triple Stroke:** The value of developing an effective triple stroke roll (RRRLLL) can't be underestimated. Triple-stroke rolls are not only the basis for some essential rudiments (flam accent #1 and flam tap), but are used extensively in rock, funk, jazz, and Latin drumset playing.

   While Moeller 3s use a technique that controls each bounce, triple strokes use a free bounce concept. In a free bounce, the tip of the stick bounces off the head some number of times (in this case, three times), and then the fingers squeeze the stick to stop it from bouncing again. In other words, triple strokes are BZZzz's that are stopped by the fingers after three bounces.

10. **Finger Control:** These exercises are designed to strengthen the small muscles in your hands that control the movement of your fingers. Using either the French grip (thumb on top of the stick) or American grip (thumb slightly off to the side) will enable the fingers to move freely. Do your best to immobilize the wrists, so that the fingers (and muscles in the hands) are given the best possible workout.

In this finger exercise, the stick is held near the tip end, and the fingers initiate the motion of the sticks, so that the butt (back end) of the stick hits the fleshy part of the underside of the forearm.

11. **Famous Stickings:** These stickings are borrowed from some of the all-time greats in the drumming world. If you practice these enough, you may become the next Stanton Moore, Steve Gadd, or Philly Joe Jones. If not, you will at least impress your friends and family with some cool-sounding stuff on the practice pad.

12. **Odd Time:** Playing in time signatures other than 4/4 and 6/8 can feel rather foreign to percussionists from Western European traditions. By playing these exercises repeatedly on one surface, you will gain confidence in handling odd-time signatures.

TIPS ON HOW BEST TO USE THE BOOK

The following list of recommendations will help you to get the most out of *Daily Drum Warm-Ups*.

Play with Your Hands

All of the included warm-up exercises (except BZZzz's) can be played with the hands on any available surface, though your legs might be the quietest option. The good news, besides the fact that you don't need a pair of sticks, is that you won't be wasting your time. By playing with your hands in the following ways, you will develop skills/techniques as if there were sticks in your hands.

Tap: Bounce off a surface with the underside of your fingers from the tips of your fingers to the padded part of your hand behind the knuckles.

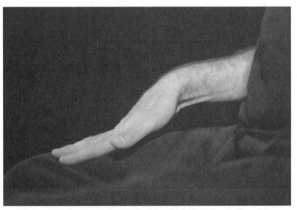

This is an unaccented note. Your fingers may feel more comfortable close together or spread apart.

Downstroke: Bounce off a surface with the entire underside of the hand.

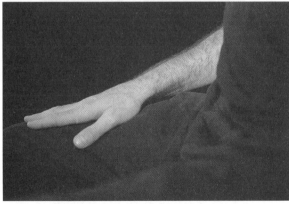

This is an accented note. Notice that the wrist has bent using a Moeller/whipping motion.

Double Strokes: Use a combination of downstroke/upstroke per hand.

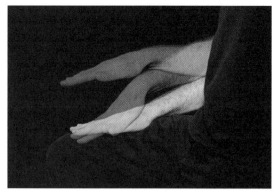

Notice the similarity between this motion and the motion as played with sticks. (See previous section called "Rudiments, Hybrid Rudiments, and Simple Patterns.")

WARNING: Neither the author nor Hal Leonard Corporation is responsible for lost wages or bad grades if you decide to warm up using your hands at the office or in school.

Play with Brushes

One of the best tools that you can buy for warming up is a pair of brushes. Brushes are generally quieter than sticks, help build touch in your playing, promote muscle development in the forearms, and provide a jazzy sound. The following basic brush techniques can be used to play the exercises in *Daily Drum Warm-Ups*.

Singles: Unaccented Notes

Taps: Bounce the top portion of the wire strands off the playing surface.

The same as using sticks, the fingers and wrist provide the energy to generate the tap.

Circle Sweeps: Sweep the top half of the wire strands in small ovals. Position the brushes according to the following photo.

Circle sweeps can be led by the right or left brush. For faster sweeps, make smaller ovals.

Side Sweeps: Four-inch brush strokes sweep toward the player in an X-shaped configuration. Once the brush finishes its sweep, it lifts barely off the playing surface and returns back to the initial position.

Notice that the brushes barely avoid contact with one another. Side sweeps can begin with either brush and could be played in an opposite manner with the brushes sweeping away from the player.

Windshield Wipers: Starting in the same position as Side Sweeps, this technique involves diagonal sweeps and return sweeps with each brush.

Once the brush has finished its diagonal sweep in one direction, it lifts off the playing surface before sweeping in the opposite direction. Observe the point at which the brushes cross but don't touch each other.

Running in Place: The top portion of the wire strands are pressed into the head and then brought up by the wrist before the next stroke. This produces a muffled sound. (The accented version of this technique is called a "plop." See following section on accented singles.)

This type of sound can create a dramatic, forward-moving effect for the listener.

Singles: Accented Notes

Rubber Shots: The rubber handle, at about two inches from the bottom of the wire strands, bounces off the rim at the same time that the top portion of the wire strands bounces off the center of the playing surface.

This might be the loudest sound that a brush can produce.

NOTE: *Most, but not all, brushes use rubber handles. They also come in wood and aluminum.*

Plops: The entire length of the wire strands lay into the head to produce this muffled accent. Plops can occur after a straight up and down motion or at anytime during a circular or sideways sweep.

The Plop is used quite often in rock or country music to produce a backbeat.

Wire Shots: The middle portion of wire strands bounce off the rim at the same time that the bottom portion bounces off the playing surface about two inches from the rim.

Wire Shots are higher in pitch than Rubber Shots.

Accelerated Sweeps: By moving faster across the playing surface, these large diagonal or oval sweeps are slightly louder and higher in pitch than Side or Circle Sweeps. They are most commonly used to accent Circle Sweeps and Taps.

Doubles: Three Types

Doubles off Strands: The top portion of the wire strands bounces twice off the playing surface. The fingers release/squeeze the brush handle to produce the double.

Doubles with Rubber: The entire wire strand portion and the very top part of the rubber handle bounce simultaneously off the head. Again, the fingers control the bounce.

Doubles as Rubber Shots: The top portion of the brush strands and the rubber handle (at about two inches from the top) bounce together two times off the head.

NOTE: *On tracks 74–78, you will find audio demonstrations of each brush technique (alternating strokes, not doubles), each played as one accent pattern. The music notation for the accent pattern can be found on page 65.*

Use Foot Ostinatos: As mentioned previously, there are 20 right foot/left foot ostinatos offered in *Daily Drum Warm-Ups*. When combined with any of the hand exercises in the book, these provide many four-limb warm-up possibilities and help develop drumset coordination. The music notation for these ostinatos is found on page 65. Listening examples can be found on audio tracks 54–73.

There are generally three techniques to play the bass drum pedal and three techniques to play the hi-hat stand. You can apply any combinations of these techniques listed on the following page, though combining certain bass drum and hi-hat techniques will affect your balance and may necessitate a change in drum throne height, bass drum pedal spring tension, position of your foot on the bass drum pedal footboard, angle of the bottom hi-hat cymbal, and distance between the top and bottom hi-hats.

Bass Drum Pedal Technique

Heel Down: The entire bottom of the foot stays on the pedal as small muscles in the foot and ankle provide the energy to push down the footboard. This technique makes it easy for the beater to come off the batter head, producing a warmer tone.

Lifting the foot off the footboard provides no mechanical advantage.

Heel Up/Bury-the-Beater: Lifting from the knee, the heel rises off the pedal, while the ball of the foot remains. The beater strikes and stays on the head, creating a muffled tone and compressed sound.

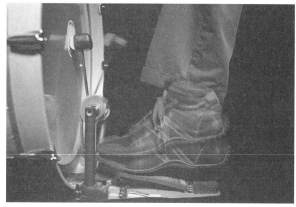

To help absorb the beater waggle, caused by the spring tension of the bass drum pedal, the batter head should be tuned fairly loosely.

Heel Up/Bounce-the-Beater: This technique is very similar to burying the beater. However, in this case, the heel drops back down during attack so that the beater bounces off the head.

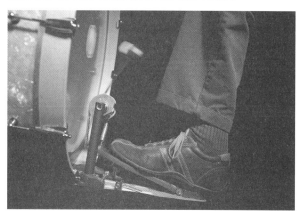

Experiment with positioning the foot down the footboard. This helps the beater bounce off the batter head when using a heel-up technique.

Hi Hat Technique

Heel Down: Similar to the Heel Down bass drum technique, the bottom of the foot remains on the footboard during the entire stroke. Small muscles control the motion.

Heel Down with Rocking: This technique uses a rocking motion between the heel and the toes. The toes lift slightly while the heel remains on, then the heel lifts slightly off the footboard and the toes land back down on the footboard. The downstroke produces a "chick" sound, while the return upstroke makes a slight open hi-hat sound.

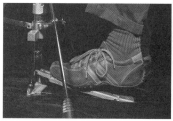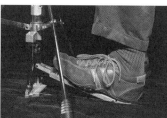

Coordination can be an issue when using the rocking motion. You have to consider the timing and coordination involved with the downstroke and the upstroke.

Heel Up: Similar to the Heel-Up/Bury-the-Beater bass drum technique, the heel remains above the footboard during the entire motion, creating a "chick sound" with a sharp attack.

Look Mom, No Pedals: Similar to playing with your hands to approximate stick work, if you tap your feet on the floor in the following ways, these techniques will simulate pedal work.

Heel Up: For softer notes, start with your heel about about one inch off the floor. Bounce your heel so that it barely touches the floor. For louder notes, start with your heel in the same position, but this time bounce the ball of your foot off the floor.

Heel Down: Start with the bottom of your foot on the floor. Keeping your heel on the ground, lift the rest of the bottom of your foot off the floor.

OTHER CONSIDERATIONS

- While playing the exercises in *Daily Drum Warm-Ups*, experiment with counting aloud, saying the stickings (R or L) aloud, or playing silently. If you decide to play silently, take the time to check your work against the Example/Audio Track. It's amazing how your brain can sometimes play tricks on you.

- Most of the exercises are written using right- and left-hand lead. Motivate yourself to try it both ways.

- Exercises can be played as short warm-ups (1–10 repetitions) or executed repeatedly until fatigue sets in (more than 10 repetitions). Besides playing the exercises as written, individual measures could be played over and over again, the order of the measures could be changed or reversed, and individual exercises could be strung together to form longer warm-ups.

- If you don't have one already, consider buying a metronome. Experiment with how you use the metronome. Besides using it in the standard way (setting it to the quarter notes), play to the whole note, to the half note, to off-beat eighth notes, etc.

- The exercises in *Daily Drum Warm-Ups* come with tempo recommendations. These are a range of tempos in which each exercise can be played comfortably.

- Try playing the exercises along with your favorite music. Dance music seems to work best for this purpose, because it normally has an easily discernible beat. Since popular music comes in many different tempos and often has a quantized beat, you'll be providing yourself with a fun, varied, and metronomic way to practice.

- Ideally, the exercises would be played on a snare drum or practice pad. The foot ostinatos would be played on a bass drum and hi-hat (or a double bass drum set-up). However, in reality, these tools are not always available. Experiment with practicing on your legs, on pillows, on the floor, etc. Have fun and use your imagination!

- Finally, all the exercises in the book were chosen so that they could easily be applied to drumset playing. If you have a chance, sit down behind a drumset, open up the book, and let your sticks fly. You'll be amazed at some of the creative ideas that you come up with.

Week 1

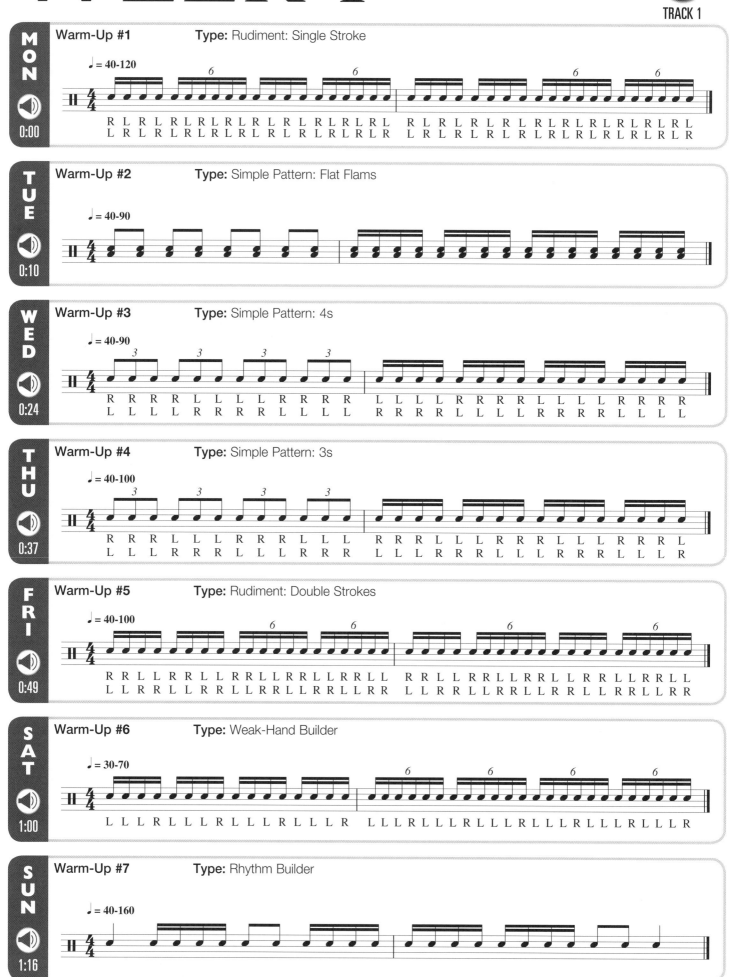

Week 2

MON — 0:00

Warm-Up #8 **Type:** Rudiment: Single Paradiddle

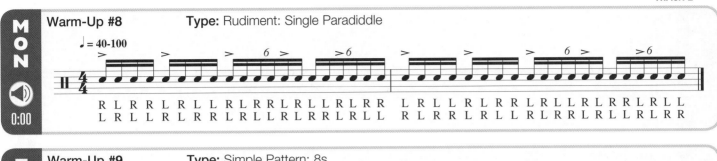

TUE — 0:11

Warm-Up #9 **Type:** Simple Pattern: 8s

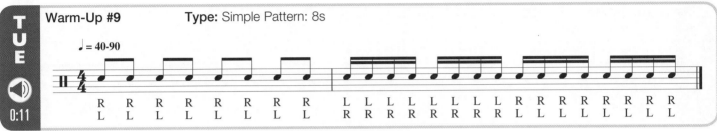

WED — 0:22

Warm-Up #10 **Type:** Rudiment: Inverted Paradiddle

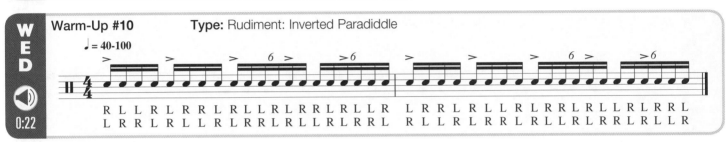

THU — 0:35

Warm-Up #11 **Type:** Simple Pattern: The 16-8 Challenge

FRI — 0:44

Warm-Up #12 **Type:** Rudiment: Alternating Flams

SAT — 0:53

Warm-Up #13 **Type:** Weak-Hand Builder

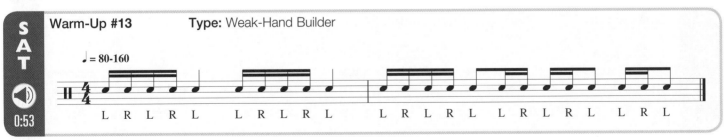

SUN — 1:02

Warm-Up #14 **Type:** Rhythm Builder

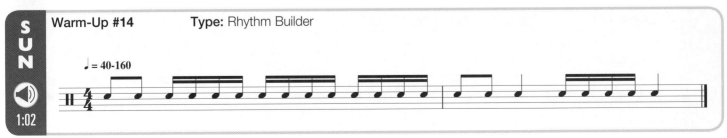

WEEK 3

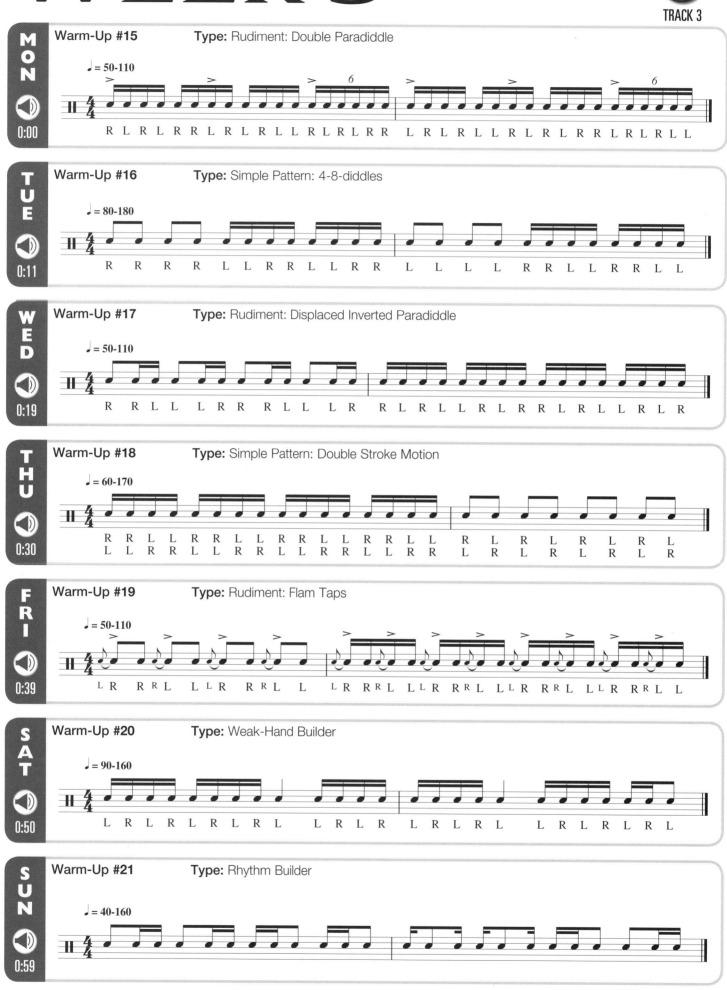

MON 0:00

Warm-Up #15   **Type:** Rudiment: Double Paradiddle

♩ = 50-110

R L R L R R L R L R L L R L R L R R   L R L R L L R L R L R R L R L R L L

TUE 0:11

Warm-Up #16   **Type:** Simple Pattern: 4-8-diddles

♩ = 80-180

R   R   R   R   L L R R L L R R   L   L   L   L   R R L L R R L L

WED 0:19

Warm-Up #17   **Type:** Rudiment: Displaced Inverted Paradiddle

♩ = 50-110

R R L L L R R R L L L R   R L R L L R L R R L R L L R L R

THU 0:30

Warm-Up #18   **Type:** Simple Pattern: Double Stroke Motion

♩ = 60-170

R R L L R R L L R R L L R R L L   R   L   R   L   R   L   R   L
L L R R L L R R L L R R L L R R   L   R   L   R   L   R   L   R

FRI 0:39

Warm-Up #19   **Type:** Rudiment: Flam Taps

♩ = 50-110

ʟR R ʳL L ʟR R ʳL L   ʟR R ʳL L ʟR R ʳL L ʟR R ʳL L ʟR R ʳL L

SAT 0:50

Warm-Up #20   **Type:** Weak-Hand Builder

♩ = 90-160

L R L R L R L R L   L R L R   L R L R L   L R L R L R L

SUN 0:59

Warm-Up #21   **Type:** Rhythm Builder

♩ = 40-160

WEEK 4

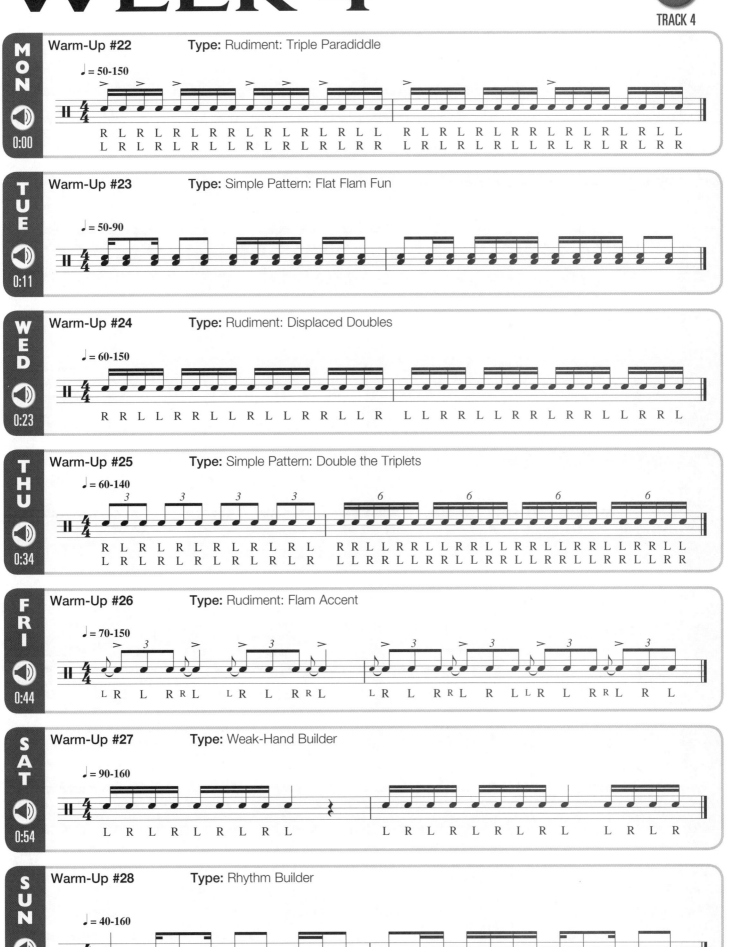

WEEK 5

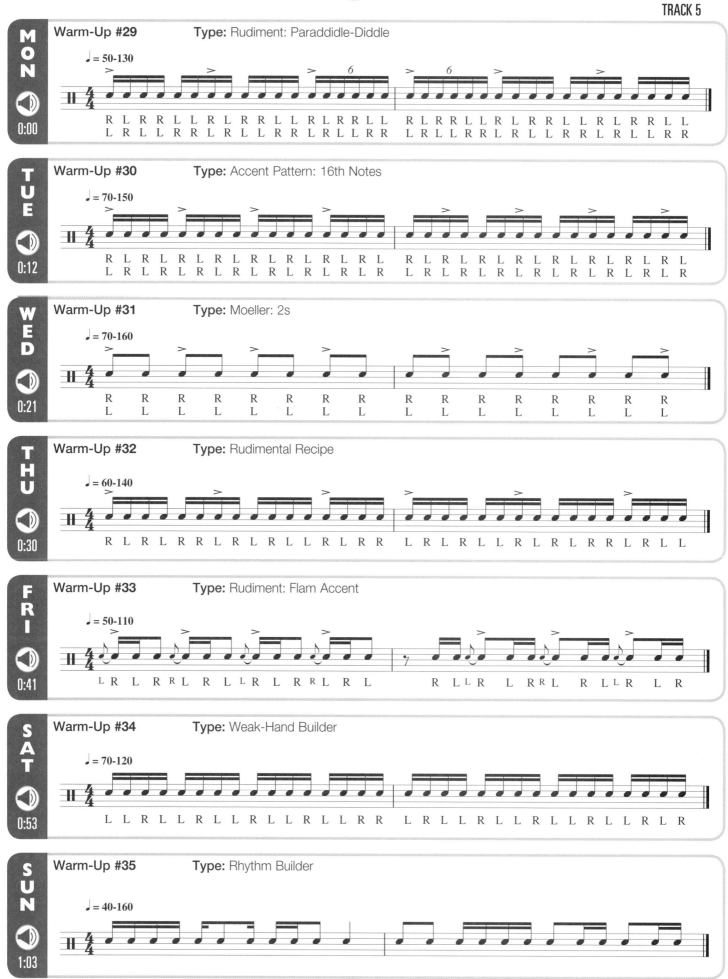

MON 0:00

Warm-Up #29   **Type:** Rudiment: Paraddidle-Diddle

♩ = 50-130

R L R R L L R L R R L L R L R R L L   R L R R L L R L R R L L R L R R L L
L R L L R R L R L L R R L R L L R R   L R L L R R L R L L R R L R L L R R

TUE 0:12

Warm-Up #30   **Type:** Accent Pattern: 16th Notes

♩ = 70-150

R L R L R L R L R L R L R L R L   R L R L R L R L R L R L R L R L
L R L R L R L R L R L R L R L R   L R L R L R L R L R L R L R L R

WED 0:21

Warm-Up #31   **Type:** Moeller: 2s

♩ = 70-160

R R R R R R R R   R R R R R R R R
L L L L L L L L   L L L L L L L L

THU 0:30

Warm-Up #32   **Type:** Rudimental Recipe

♩ = 60-140

R L R L R R L R L R L L R L R R   L R L R L L R L R L R R L R L L

FRI 0:41

Warm-Up #33   **Type:** Rudiment: Flam Accent

♩ = 50-110

ʟR L R Rʟ R L R Lʟ R L R Rʟ R L   R ʟʟR L Rʀ L R ʟʟR L R

SAT 0:53

Warm-Up #34   **Type:** Weak-Hand Builder

♩ = 70-120

L L R L L R L L R L L R L L R R   L R L L R L L R L L R L L R L R

SUN 1:03

Warm-Up #35   **Type:** Rhythm Builder

♩ = 40-160

WEEK 6

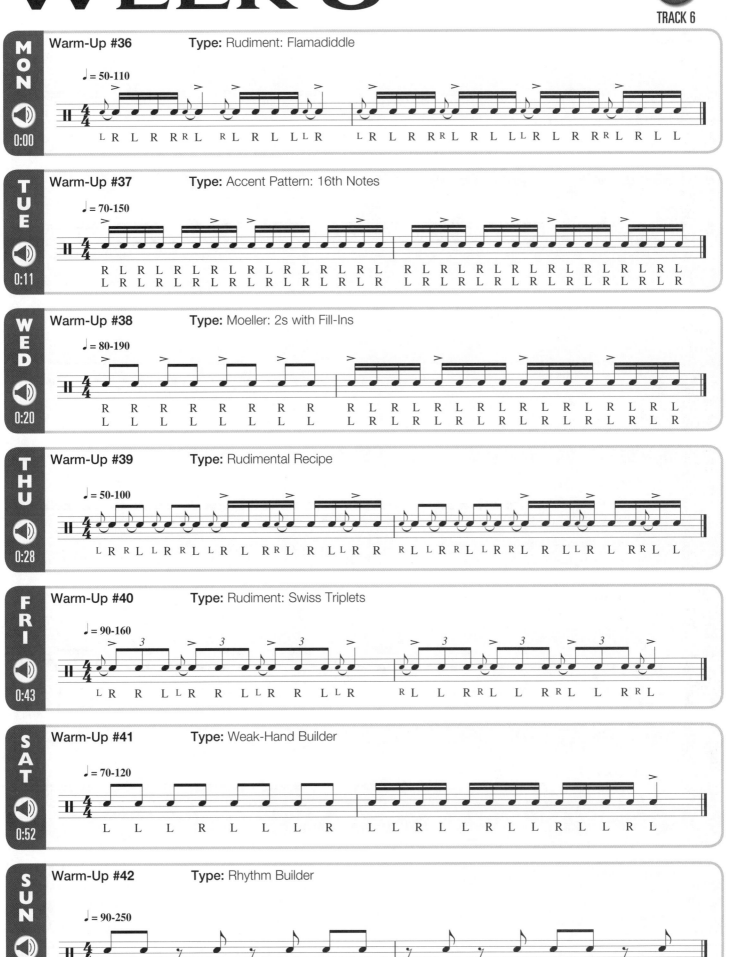

Week 7

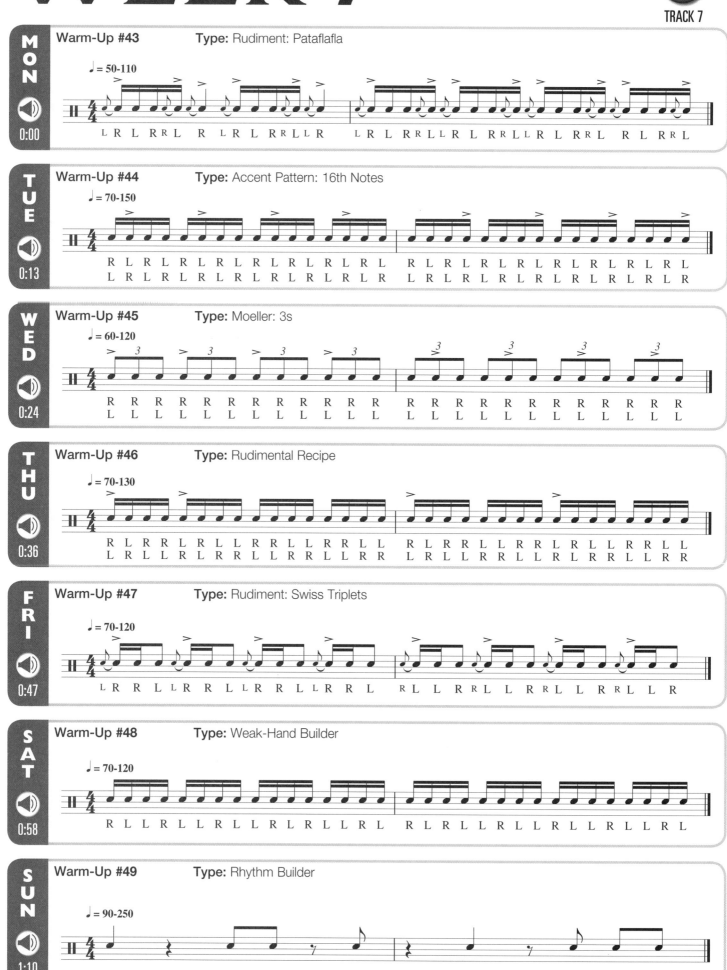

Week 8

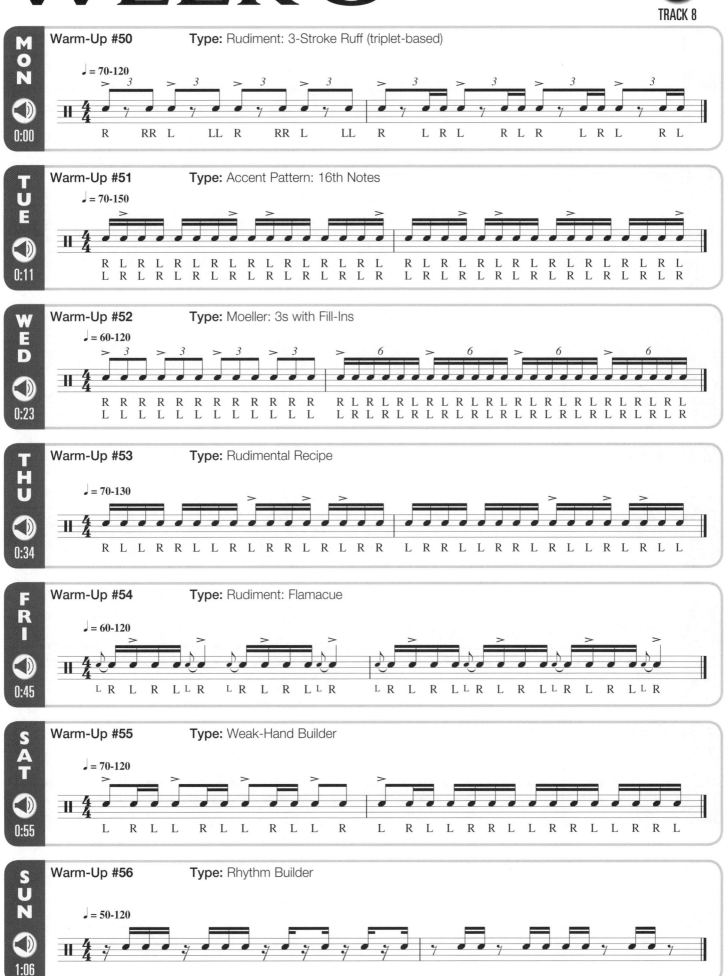

MON 0:00

Warm-Up #50   **Type:** Rudiment: 3-Stroke Ruff (triplet-based)

♩ = 70-120

R RR L LL R RR L LL R L R L R L R L R L R L

TUE 0:11

Warm-Up #51   **Type:** Accent Pattern: 16th Notes

♩ = 70-150

R L R L R L R L R L R L R L R L R L R L R L R L R L R L R L R L
L R L R L R L R L R L R L R L R L R L R L R L R L R L R L R L R

WED 0:23

Warm-Up #52   **Type:** Moeller: 3s with Fill-Ins

♩ = 60-120

R R R R R R R R R R R R RL RL RL RL RL RL RL RL RL RL RL RL
L L L L L L L L L L L L LR LR LR LR LR LR LR LR LR LR LR LR

THU 0:34

Warm-Up #53   **Type:** Rudimental Recipe

♩ = 70-130

R L L R R L L R L R R L R L R R L R R L L R R L R L L R L R L L

FRI 0:45

Warm-Up #54   **Type:** Rudiment: Flamacue

♩ = 60-120

L R L R LL R L R L R LL R L R L R LL R L R L R LL R L R L R LL R

SAT 0:55

Warm-Up #55   **Type:** Weak-Hand Builder

♩ = 70-120

L R L L R L L R L L R L R L L R R L L R R L L R R L

SUN 1:06

Warm-Up #56   **Type:** Rhythm Builder

♩ = 50-120

Week 9

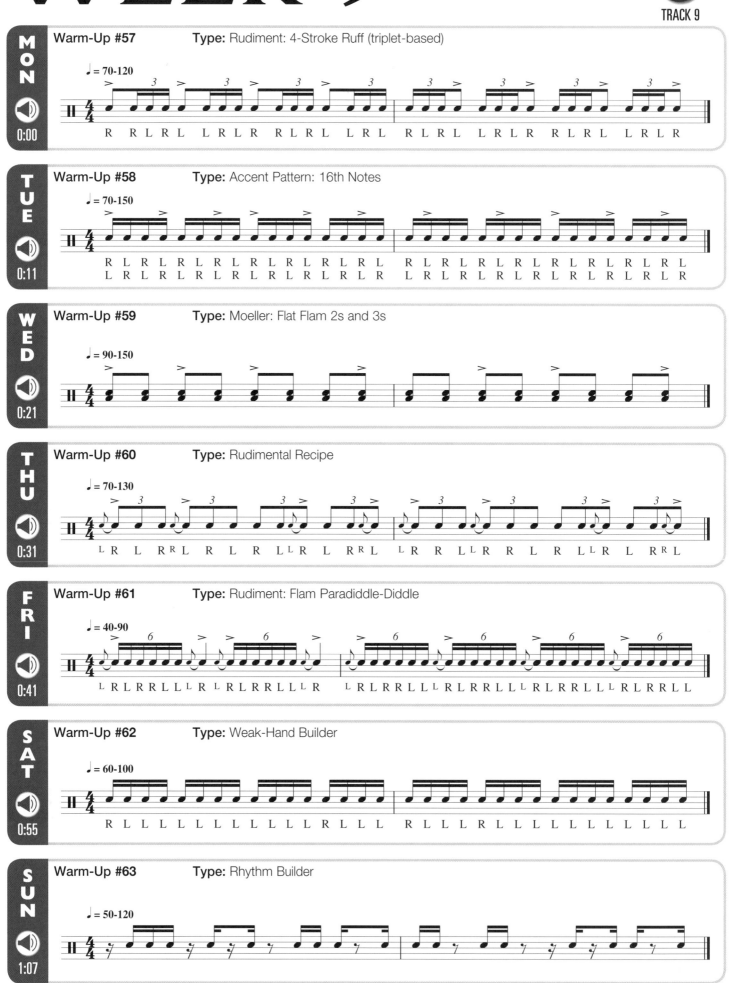

MON 0:00

Warm-Up #57 **Type:** Rudiment: 4-Stroke Ruff (triplet-based)

♩ = 70-120

R R L R L L R L R L R L L R L R L R L L R L R L R L R L L R L R

TUE 0:11

Warm-Up #58 **Type:** Accent Pattern: 16th Notes

♩ = 70-150

R L R L R L R L R L R L R L R L R L R L R L R L R L R L R L R L
L R L R L R L R L R L R L R L R L R L R L R L R L R L R L R L R

WED 0:21

Warm-Up #59 **Type:** Moeller: Flat Flam 2s and 3s

♩ = 90-150

THU 0:31

Warm-Up #60 **Type:** Rudimental Recipe

♩ = 70-130

L R L R R L R L R L L R L R R L L R R L L R R L R L R L L R R L

FRI 0:41

Warm-Up #61 **Type:** Rudiment: Flam Paradiddle-Diddle

♩ = 40-90

L R L R R L L L R L R L R R L L L R L R L R R L L R L R R L L L R L R R L L L R L R R L L

SAT 0:55

Warm-Up #62 **Type:** Weak-Hand Builder

♩ = 60-100

R L L L L L L L L L L L R L L L R L L L R L L L L L L L L L L L

SUN 1:07

Warm-Up #63 **Type:** Rhythm Builder

♩ = 50-120

Week 10

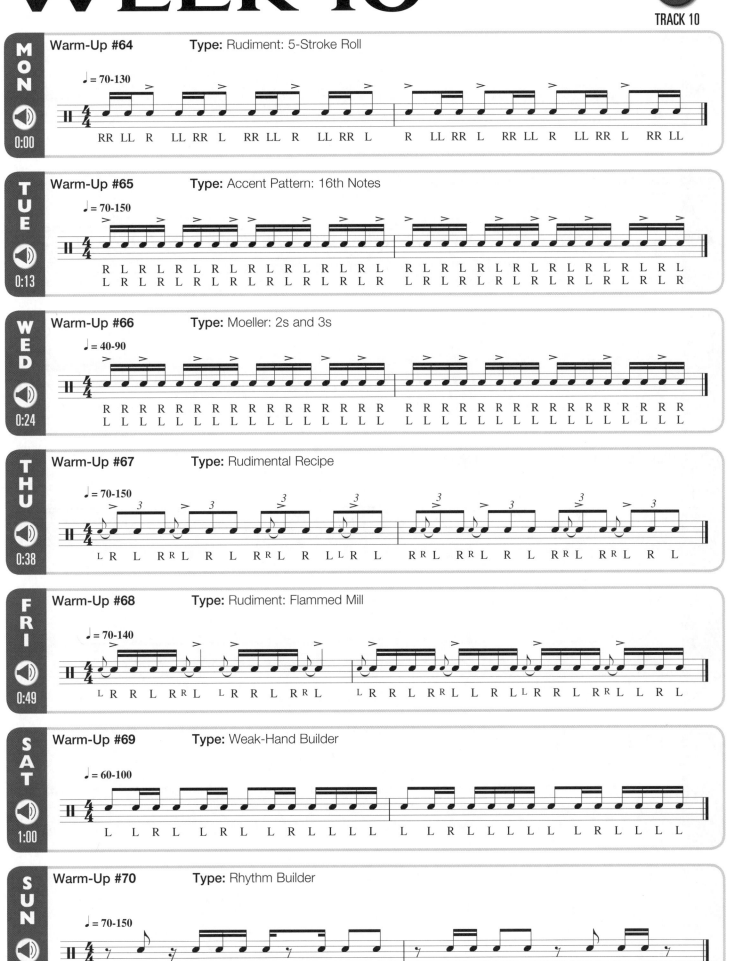

MON 0:00 — **Warm-Up #64** **Type:** Rudiment: 5-Stroke Roll

TUE 0:13 — **Warm-Up #65** **Type:** Accent Pattern: 16th Notes

WED 0:24 — **Warm-Up #66** **Type:** Moeller: 2s and 3s

THU 0:38 — **Warm-Up #67** **Type:** Rudimental Recipe

FRI 0:49 — **Warm-Up #68** **Type:** Rudiment: Flammed Mill

SAT 1:00 — **Warm-Up #69** **Type:** Weak-Hand Builder

SUN 1:12 — **Warm-Up #70** **Type:** Rhythm Builder

WEEK 11

TRACK 11

MON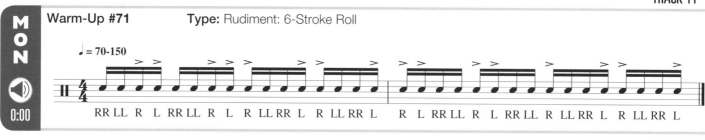
0:00

Warm-Up #71   **Type:** Rudiment: 6-Stroke Roll

♩ = 70-150

RR LL R L RR LL R L RR LL R L RR LL R L   R L RR LL R L RR LL R L RR LL R L RR L

TUE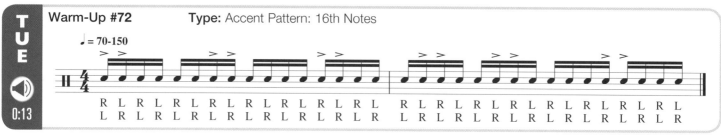
0:13

Warm-Up #72   **Type:** Accent Pattern: 16th Notes

♩ = 70-150

R L R L R L R L R L R L R L R L   R L R L R L R L R L R L R L R L
L R L R L R L R L R L R L R L R   L R L R L R L R L R L R L R L R

WED
0:25

Warm-Up #73   **Type:** Moeller: 4s

♩ = 40-90

R R R R R R R R R R R R R R R R   R R R R R R R R R R R R R R R R
L L L L L L L L L L L L L L L L   L L L L L L L L L L L L L L L L

THU
0:40

Warm-Up #74   **Type:** Rudimental Recipe

♩ = 50-110

L R L R R L R L L R L R R L L R L R R L   L R L R R L R L L R L R R L L R L R R L

FRI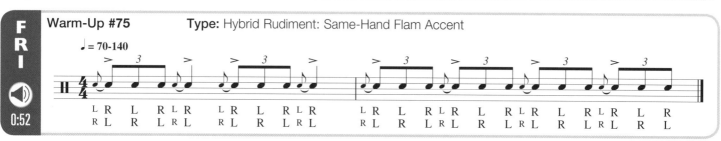
0:52

Warm-Up #75   **Type:** Hybrid Rudiment: Same-Hand Flam Accent

♩ = 70-140

L R L R L R   L R L R L R   L R L R L R L R L R L R
R L R L R L   R L R L R L   R L R L R L R L R L R L

SAT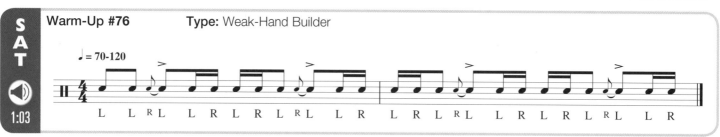
1:03

Warm-Up #76   **Type:** Weak-Hand Builder

♩ = 70-120

L L R L L R L R L R L R L   L R L R L R L R L R L R L R L R L R L R L R

SUN
1:14

Warm-Up #77   **Type:** Rhythm Builder

♩ = 60-110

Week 12

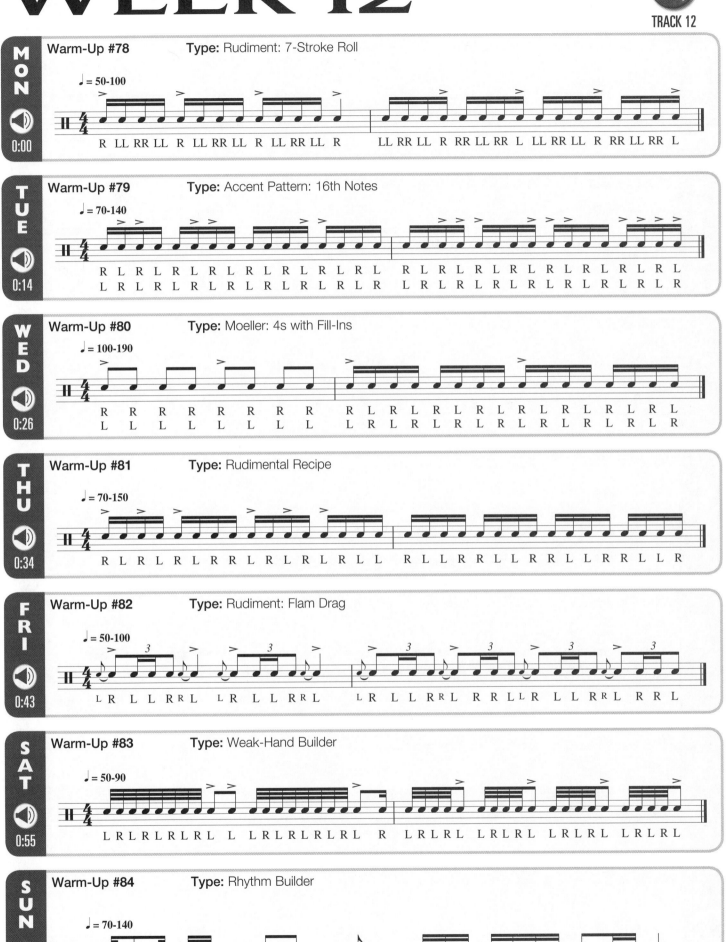

WEEK 13

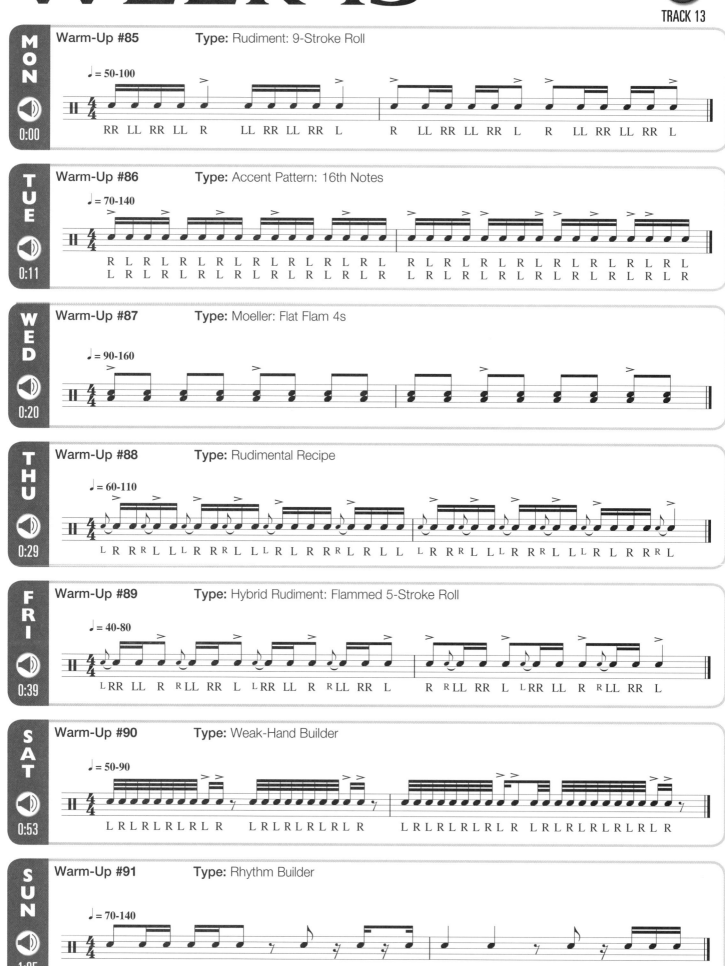

MON 0:00

Warm-Up #85 **Type:** Rudiment: 9-Stroke Roll

♩ = 50-100

RR LL RR LL R   LL RR LL RR L   R   LL RR LL RR L   R   LL RR LL RR L

TUE 0:11

Warm-Up #86 **Type:** Accent Pattern: 16th Notes

♩ = 70-140

R L R L R L R L R L R L R L R L   R L R L R L R L R L R L R L R L
L R L R L R L R L R L R L R L R   L R L R L R L R L R L R L R L R

WED 0:20

Warm-Up #87 **Type:** Moeller: Flat Flam 4s

♩ = 90-160

THU 0:29

Warm-Up #88 **Type:** Rudimental Recipe

♩ = 60-110

L R R R L L L R R L L L R L R R R L R L L   L R R R L L L R R R L L L R L R R R L

FRI 0:39

Warm-Up #89 **Type:** Hybrid Rudiment: Flammed 5-Stroke Roll

♩ = 40-80

L RR LL R R LL RR L L RR LL R R LL RR L   R R LL RR L L RR LL R R LL RR L

SAT 0:53

Warm-Up #90 **Type:** Weak-Hand Builder

♩ = 50-90

L R L R L R L R L R   L R L R L R L R L R   L R L R L R L R L R L R L R L R L R L R

SUN 1:05

Warm-Up #91 **Type:** Rhythm Builder

♩ = 70-140

24

WEEK 14

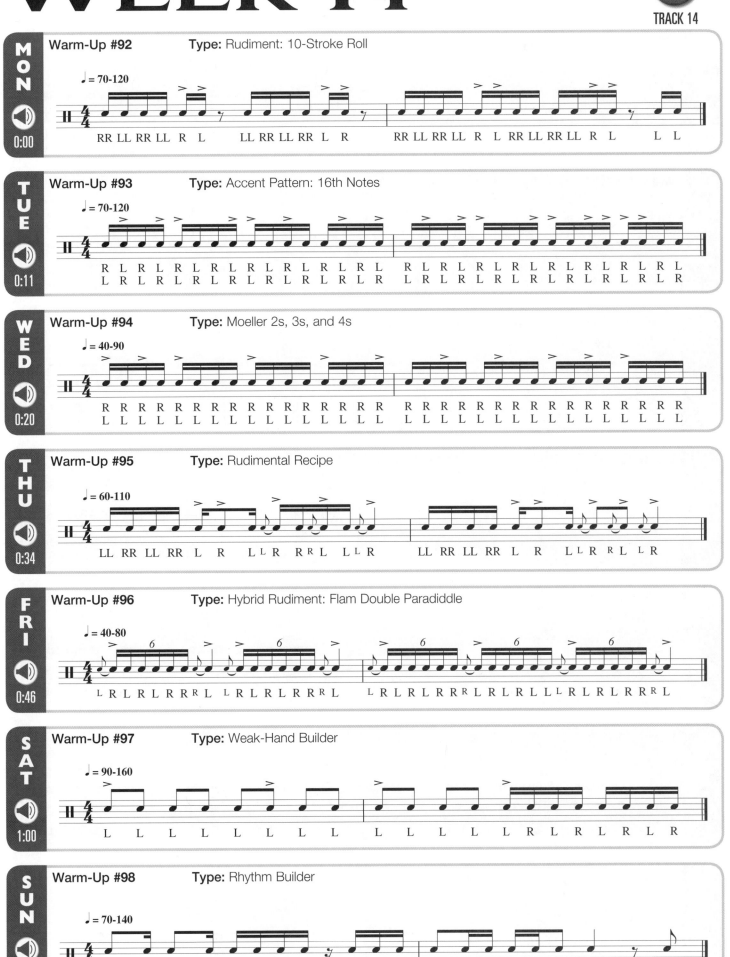

MON — 0:00 — **Warm-Up #92** **Type:** Rudiment: 10-Stroke Roll

TUE — 0:11 — **Warm-Up #93** **Type:** Accent Pattern: 16th Notes

WED — 0:20 — **Warm-Up #94** **Type:** Moeller 2s, 3s, and 4s

THU — 0:34 — **Warm-Up #95** **Type:** Rudimental Recipe

FRI — 0:46 — **Warm-Up #96** **Type:** Hybrid Rudiment: Flam Double Paradiddle

SAT — 1:00 — **Warm-Up #97** **Type:** Weak-Hand Builder

SUN — 1:10 — **Warm-Up #98** **Type:** Rhythm Builder

WEEK 15

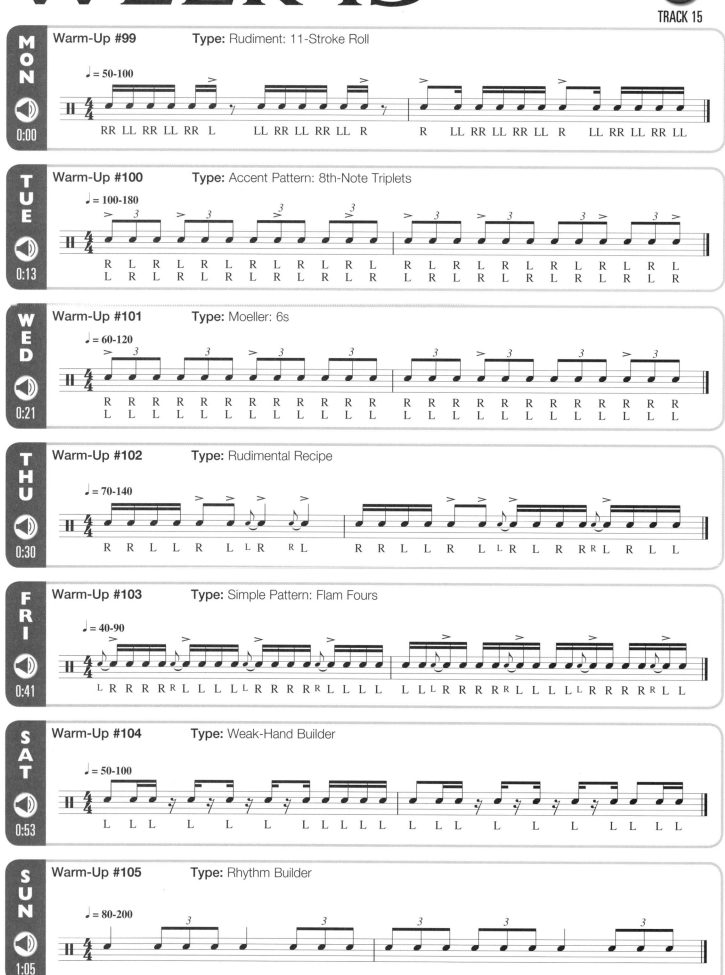

WEEK 16

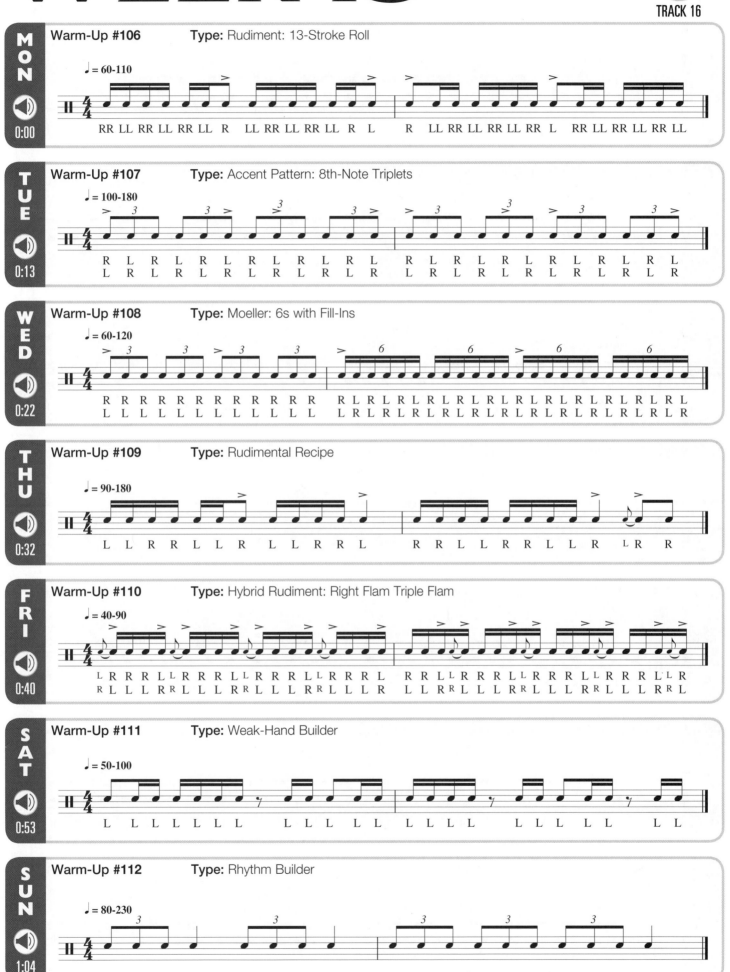

MON 0:00 — **Warm-Up #106** **Type:** Rudiment: 13-Stroke Roll

TUE 0:13 — **Warm-Up #107** **Type:** Accent Pattern: 8th-Note Triplets

WED 0:22 — **Warm-Up #108** **Type:** Moeller: 6s with Fill-Ins

THU 0:32 — **Warm-Up #109** **Type:** Rudimental Recipe

FRI 0:40 — **Warm-Up #110** **Type:** Hybrid Rudiment: Right Flam Triple Flam

SAT 0:53 — **Warm-Up #111** **Type:** Weak-Hand Builder

SUN 1:04 — **Warm-Up #112** **Type:** Rhythm Builder

Week 17

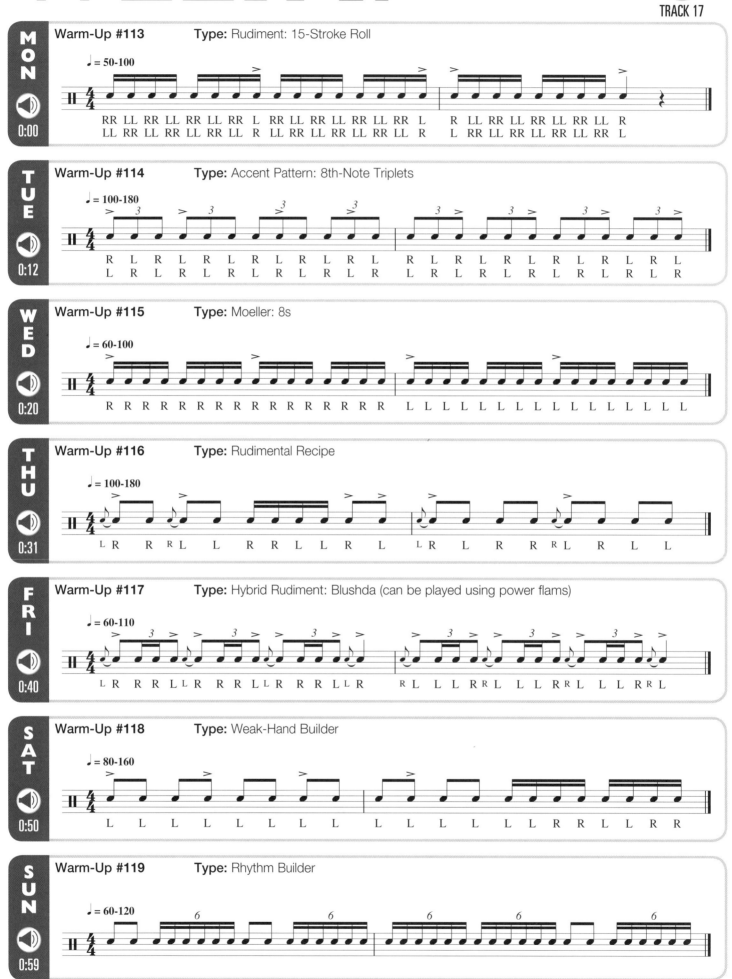

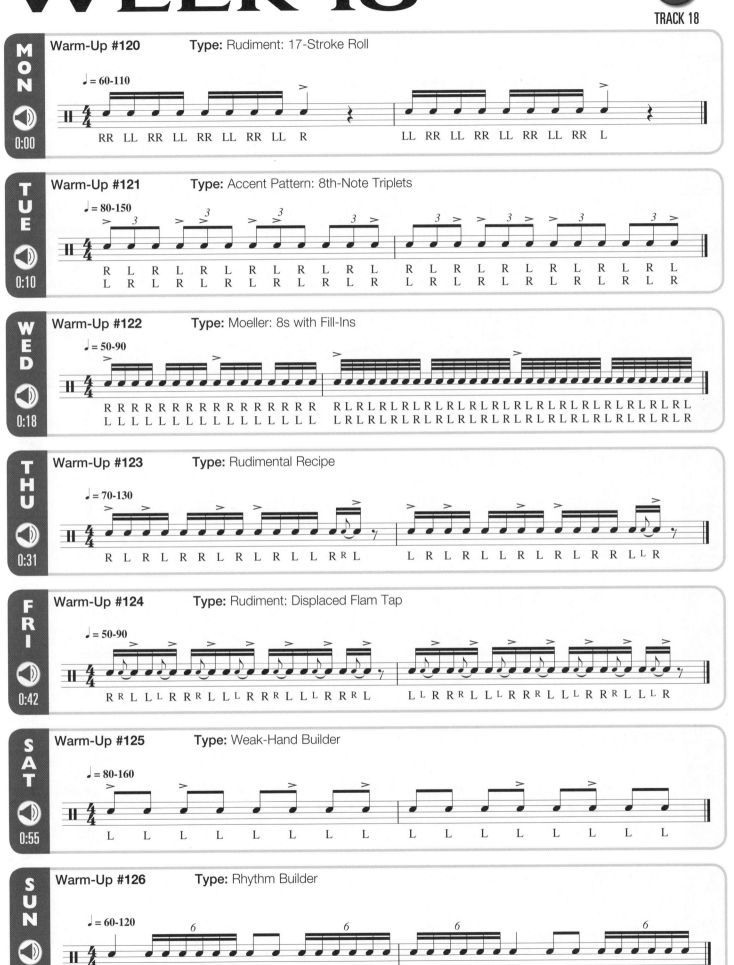

Week 19

MON 0:00

Warm-Up #127 **Type:** Rudiment: Single Drag

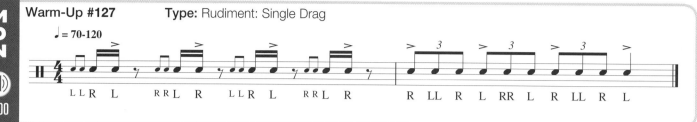

TUE 0:10

Warm-Up #128 **Type:** Accent Pattern: 8th-Note Triplets

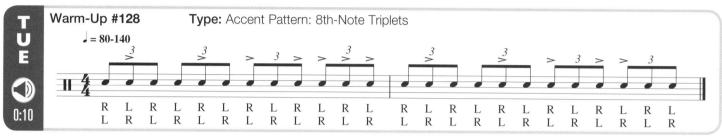

WED 0:19

Warm-Up #129 **Type:** Moeller: Overlapping 2s

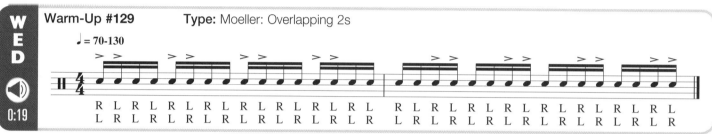

THU 0:28

Warm-Up #130 **Type:** Rudimental Recipe

FRI 0:39

Warm-Up #131 **Type:** Hybrid Rudiment: Flammed Singles Doubles

SAT 0:49

Warm-Up #132 **Type:** Weak-Hand Builder

SUN 1:01

Warm-Up #133 **Type:** Rhythm Builder

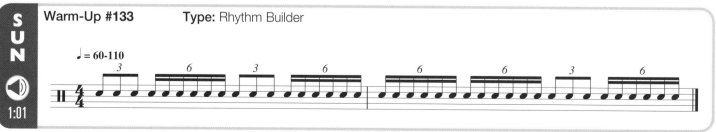

TRACK 20

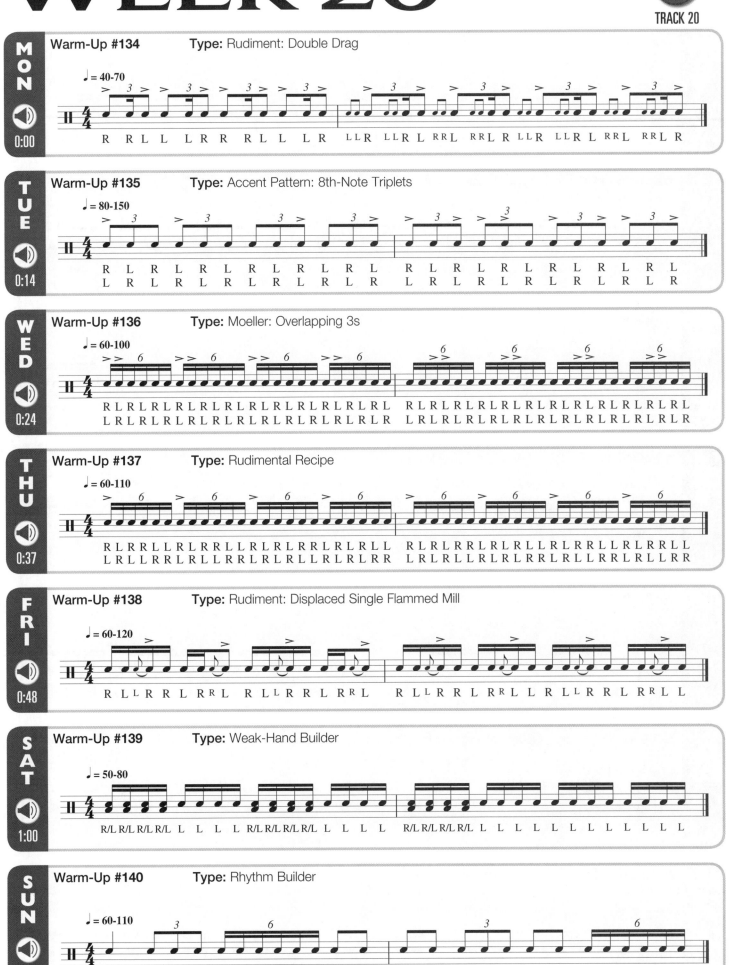

WEEK 21

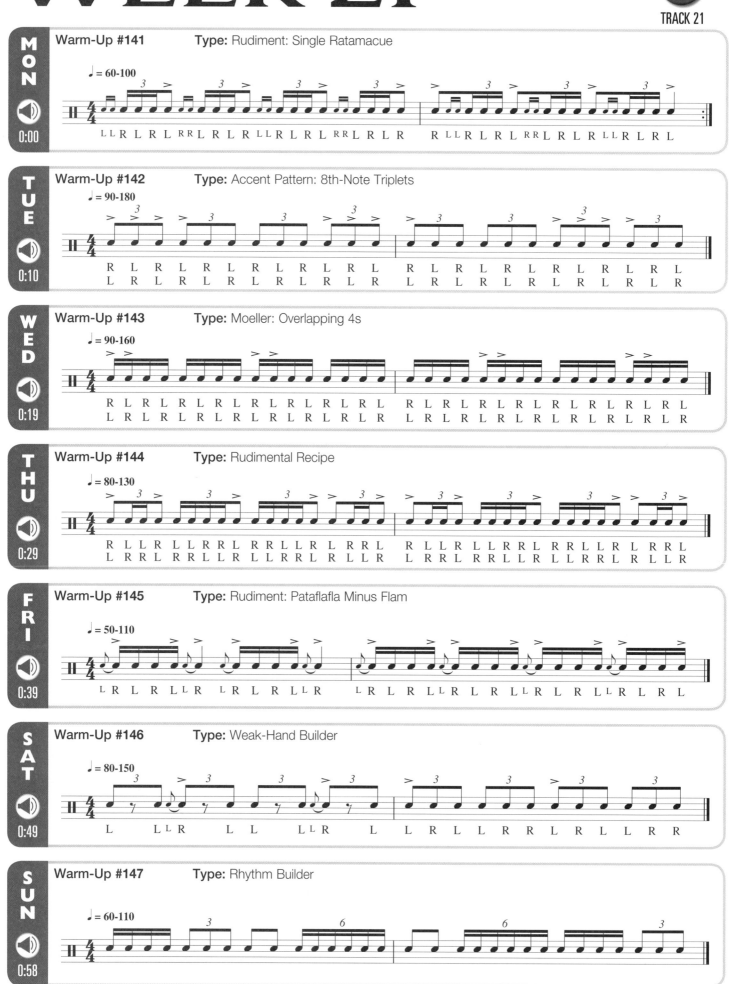

Week 22

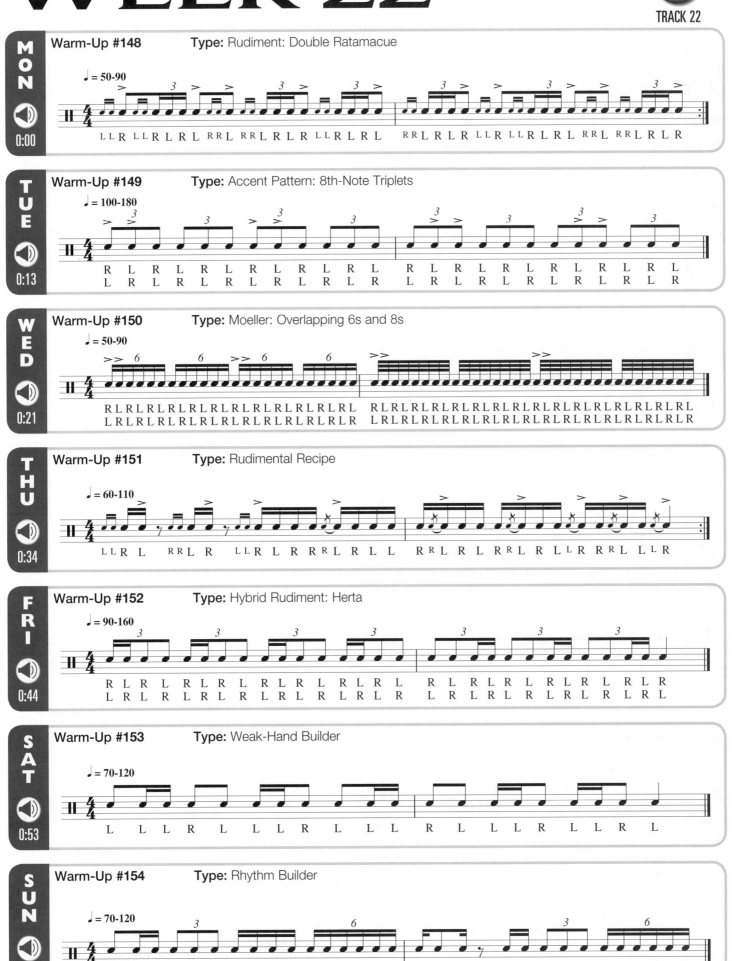

TRACK 23

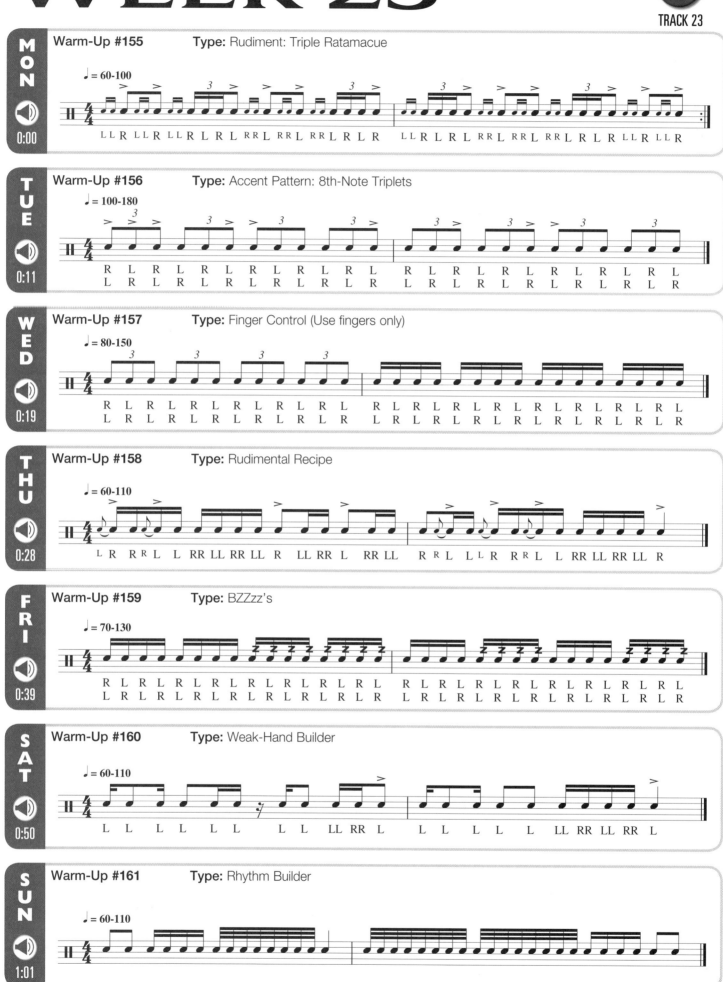

Week 24

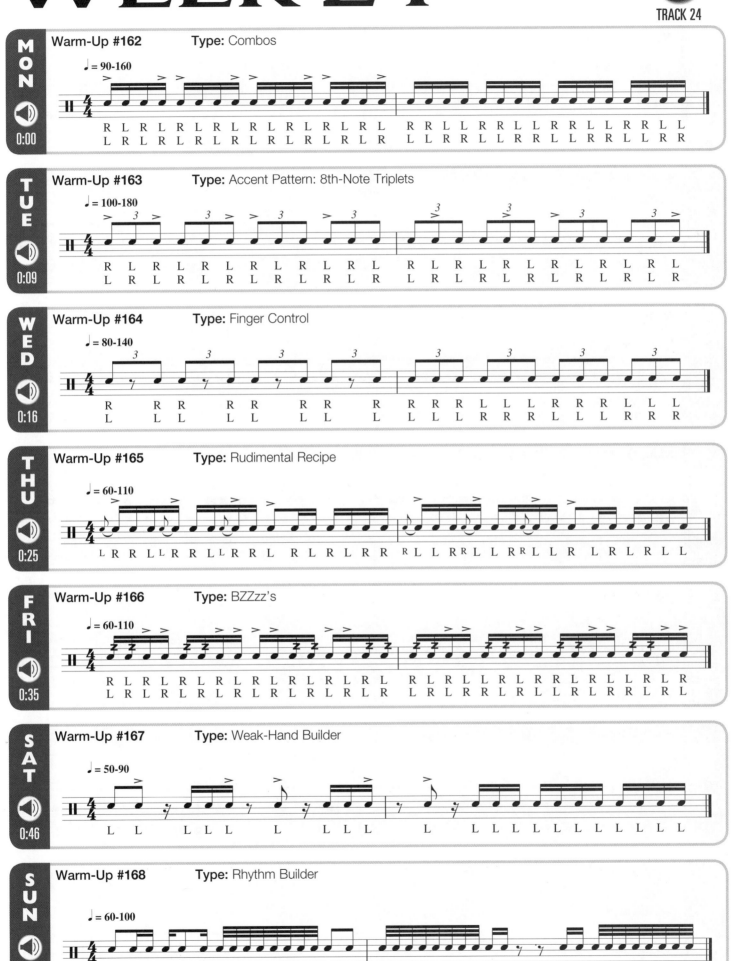

MON 0:00

Warm-Up #162 **Type:** Combos

♩ = 90-160

R L R L R L R L R L R L R L R L   R R L L R R L L R R L L R R L L
L R L R L R L R L R L R L R L R   L L R R L L R R L L R R L L R R

TUE 0:09

Warm-Up #163 **Type:** Accent Pattern: 8th-Note Triplets

♩ = 100-180

R L R L R L R L R L R L R L R L   R L R L R L R L R L R L R L R L
L R L R L R L R L R L R L R L R   L R L R L R L R L R L R L R L R

WED 0:16

Warm-Up #164 **Type:** Finger Control

♩ = 80-140

R   R R   R R   R R   R   R R R L L L R R R L L L
L   L L   L L   L L   L   L L R R R L L L R R R

THU 0:25

Warm-Up #165 **Type:** Rudimental Recipe

♩ = 60-110

L R R L L R R L L R R L   R L R L R R   R L L R R L L R R L L R   R L R L R L L

FRI 0:35

Warm-Up #166 **Type:** BZZzz's

♩ = 60-110

R L R L R L R L R L R L R L R L   R L R L L R L R R L R L L R L R
L R L R L R L R L R L R L R L R   L R L R R L R L L R L R R L R L

SAT 0:46

Warm-Up #167 **Type:** Weak-Hand Builder

♩ = 50-90

L L   L L L   L   L L L   L   L L L L L L L L L L L L

SUN 1:00

Warm-Up #168 **Type:** Rhythm Builder

♩ = 60-100

35

Week 25

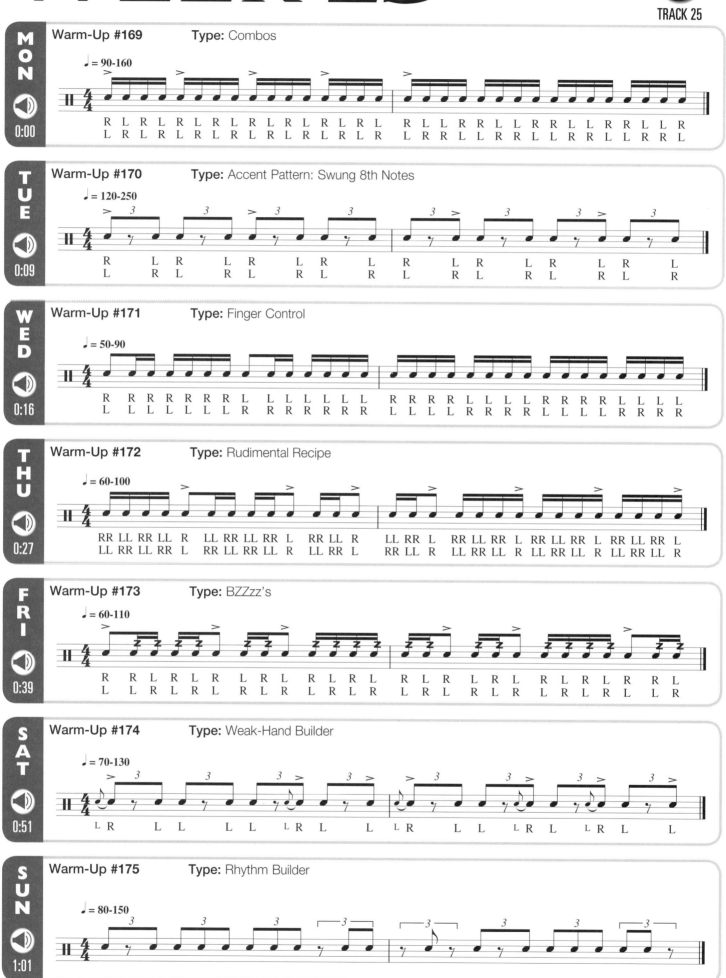

Week 26

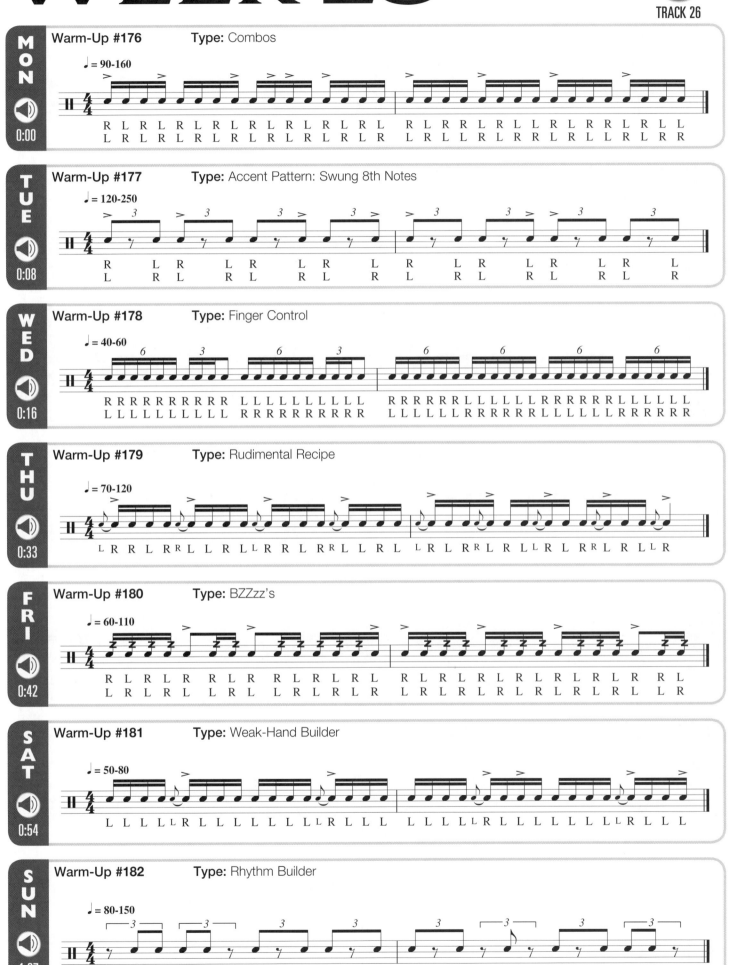

Week 27

MON 0:00

Warm-Up #183 **Type:** Combos

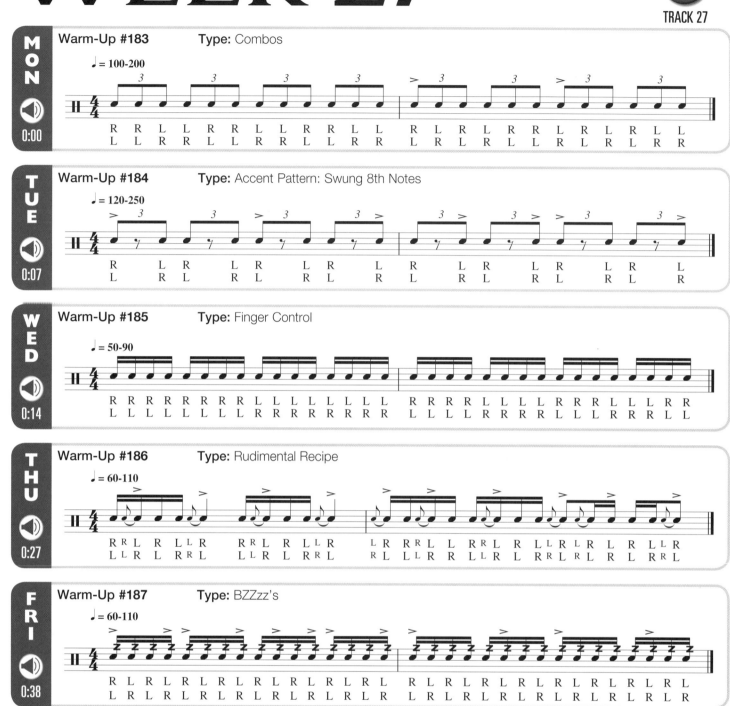

TUE 0:07

Warm-Up #184 **Type:** Accent Pattern: Swung 8th Notes

WED 0:14

Warm-Up #185 **Type:** Finger Control

THU 0:27

Warm-Up #186 **Type:** Rudimental Recipe

FRI 0:38

Warm-Up #187 **Type:** BZZzz's

SAT 0:50

Warm-Up #188 **Type:** Weak-Hand Builder

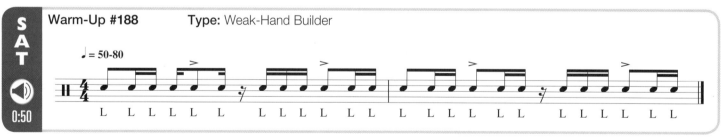

SUN 1:04

Warm-Up #189 **Type:** Rhythm Builder

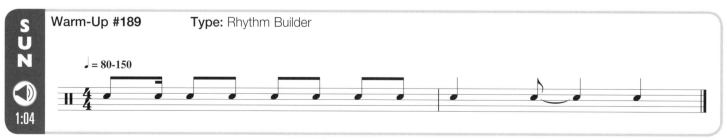

Week 28

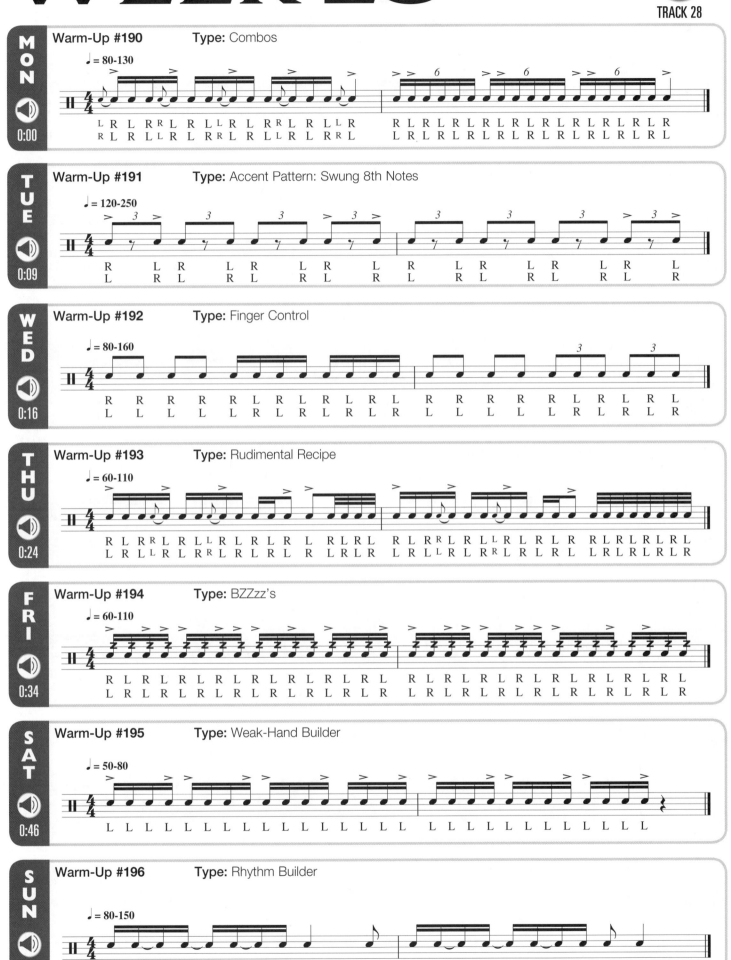

Week 29

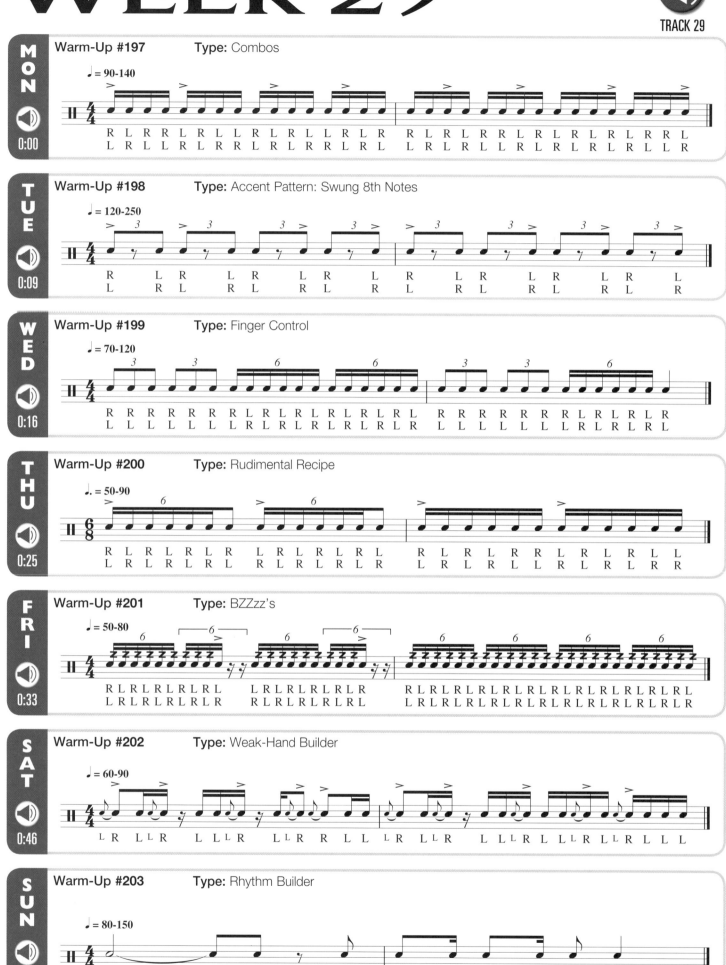

WEEK 30

MON 0:00

Warm-Up #204 **Type:** Combos

TUE 0:13

Warm-Up #205 **Type:** Accent Pattern: Swung 8th Notes

WED 0:20

Warm-Up #206 **Type:** Finger Control

THU 0:27

Warm-Up #207 **Type:** Rudimental Recipe

FRI 0:39

Warm-Up #208 **Type:** BZZzz's

SAT 0:54

Warm-Up #209 **Type:** Weak-Hand Builder

SUN 1:02

Warm-Up #210 **Type:** Rhythm Builder

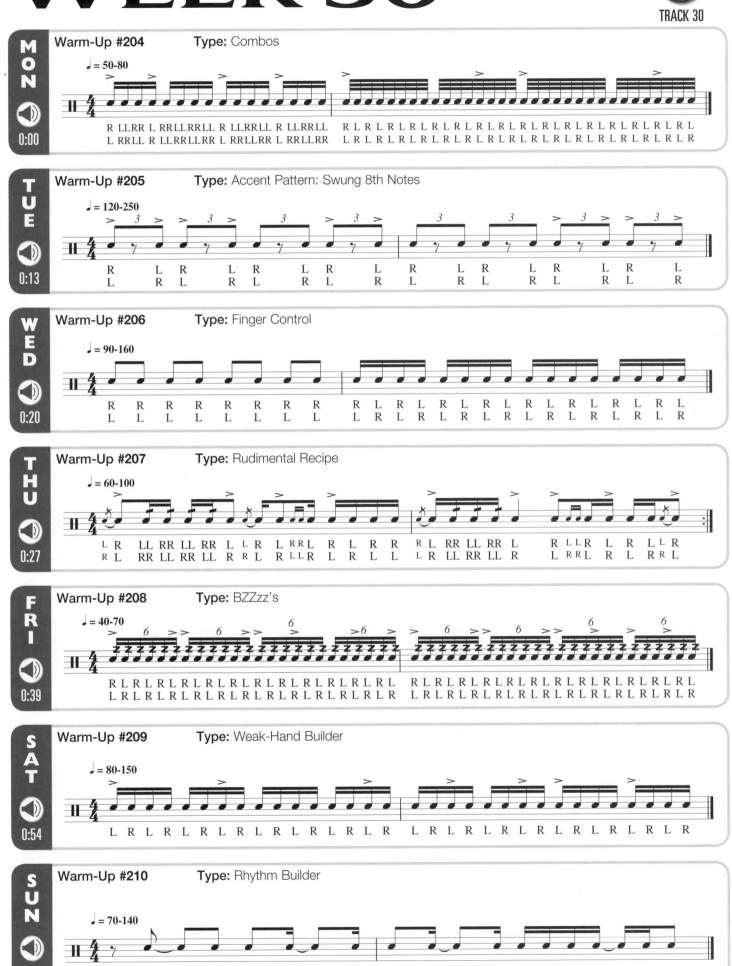

Week 31

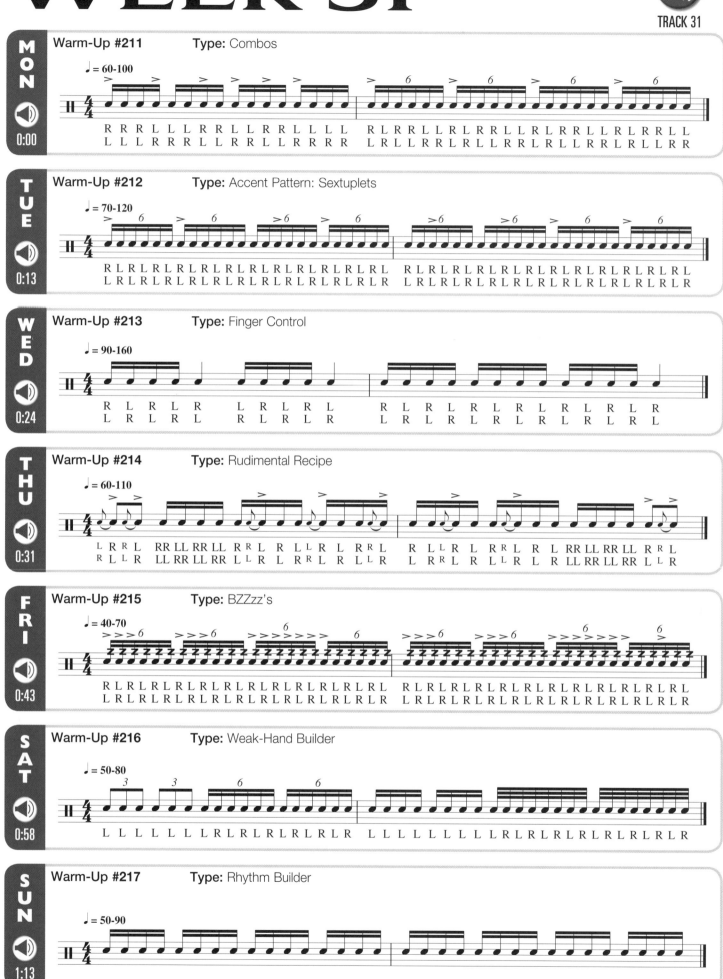

MON — Warm-Up #211 — **Type:** Combos — 0:00

TUE — Warm-Up #212 — **Type:** Accent Pattern: Sextuplets — 0:13

WED — Warm-Up #213 — **Type:** Finger Control — 0:24

THU — Warm-Up #214 — **Type:** Rudimental Recipe — 0:31

FRI — Warm-Up #215 — **Type:** BZZzz's — 0:43

SAT — Warm-Up #216 — **Type:** Weak-Hand Builder — 0:58

SUN — Warm-Up #217 — **Type:** Rhythm Builder — 1:13

WEEK 32

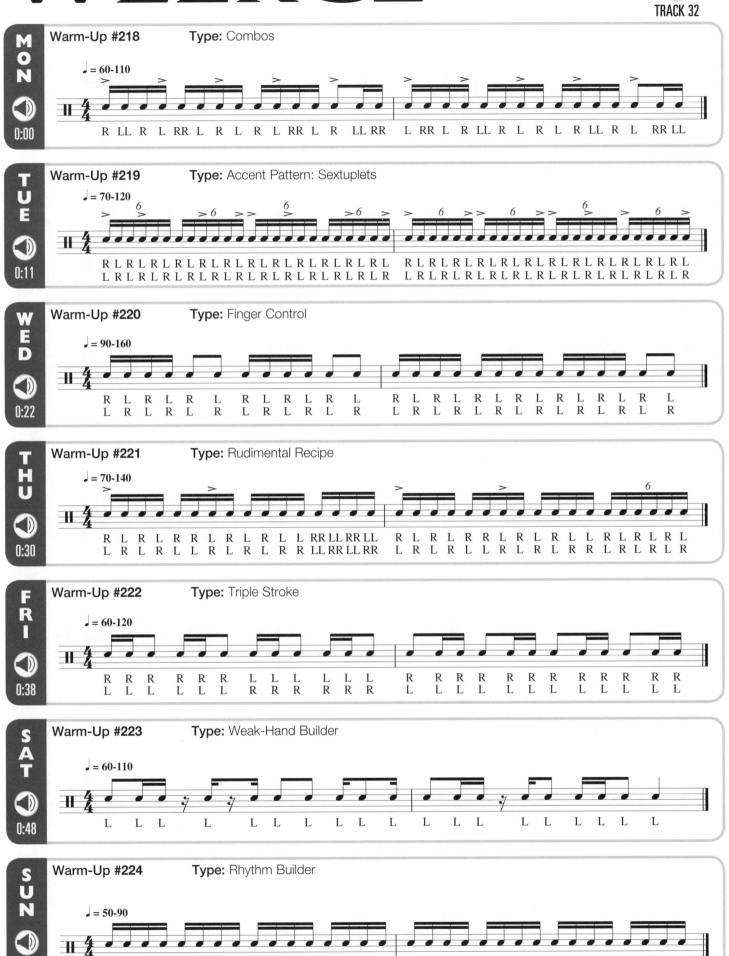

MON 0:00 — **Warm-Up #218** **Type:** Combos

TUE 0:11 — **Warm-Up #219** **Type:** Accent Pattern: Sextuplets

WED 0:22 — **Warm-Up #220** **Type:** Finger Control

THU 0:30 — **Warm-Up #221** **Type:** Rudimental Recipe

FRI 0:38 — **Warm-Up #222** **Type:** Triple Stroke

SAT 0:48 — **Warm-Up #223** **Type:** Weak-Hand Builder

SUN 0:58 — **Warm-Up #224** **Type:** Rhythm Builder

Week 33

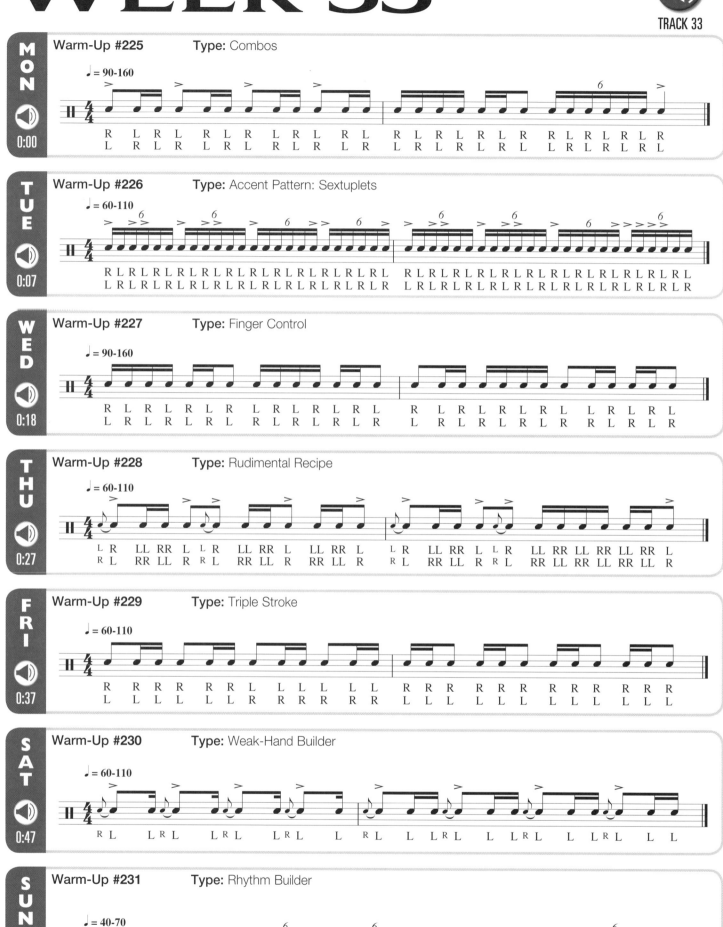

MON 0:00

Warm-Up #225 **Type:** Combos

TUE 0:07

Warm-Up #226 **Type:** Accent Pattern: Sextuplets

WED 0:18

Warm-Up #227 **Type:** Finger Control

THU 0:27

Warm-Up #228 **Type:** Rudimental Recipe

FRI 0:37

Warm-Up #229 **Type:** Triple Stroke

SAT 0:47

Warm-Up #230 **Type:** Weak-Hand Builder

SUN 0:58

Warm-Up #231 **Type:** Rhythm Builder

Week 34

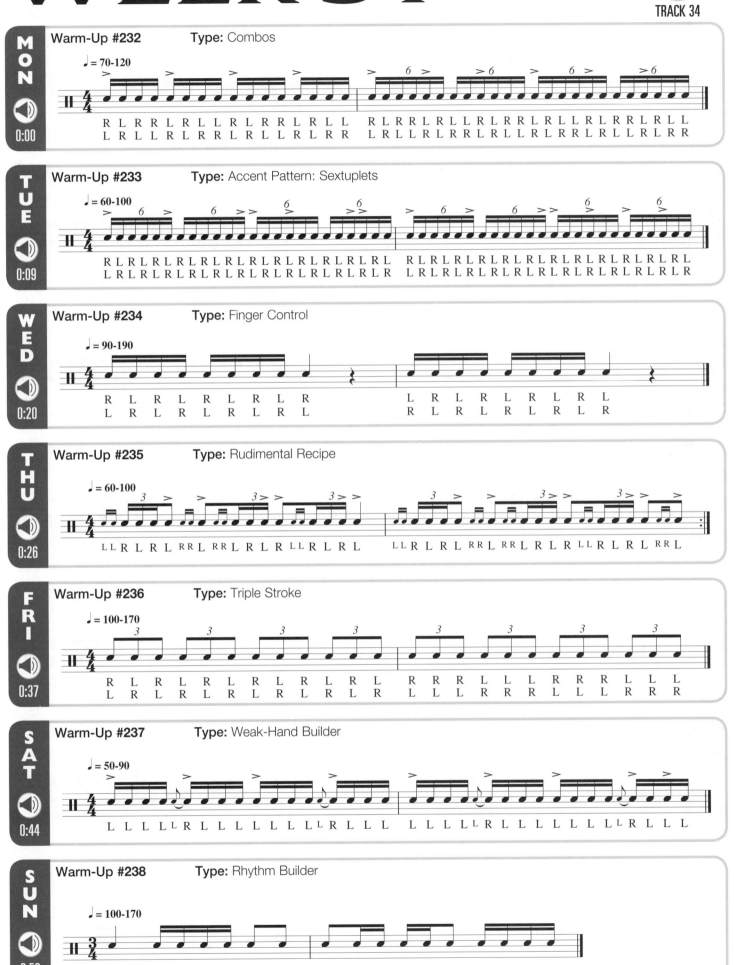

MON 0:00

Warm-Up #232　　　Type: Combos

TUE 0:09

Warm-Up #233　　　Type: Accent Pattern: Sextuplets

WED 0:20

Warm-Up #234　　　Type: Finger Control

THU 0:26

Warm-Up #235　　　Type: Rudimental Recipe

FRI 0:37

Warm-Up #236　　　Type: Triple Stroke

SAT 0:44

Warm-Up #237　　　Type: Weak-Hand Builder

SUN 0:56

Warm-Up #238　　　Type: Rhythm Builder

Week 35

MON 0:00

Warm-Up #239 **Type:** Combos

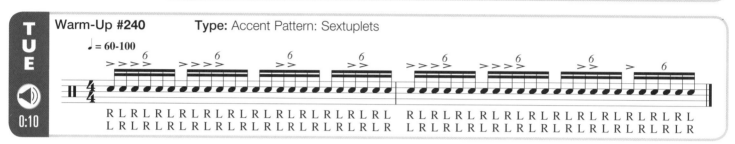

TUE 0:10

Warm-Up #240 **Type:** Accent Pattern: Sextuplets

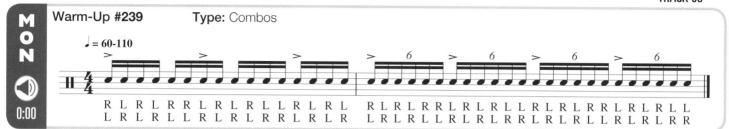

WED 0:23

Warm-Up #241 **Type:** Finger Control

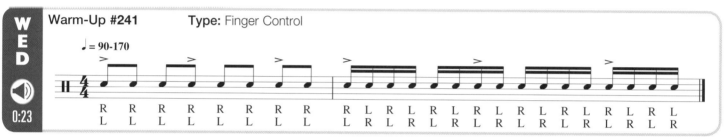

THU 0:30

Warm-Up #242 **Type:** Rudimental Recipe

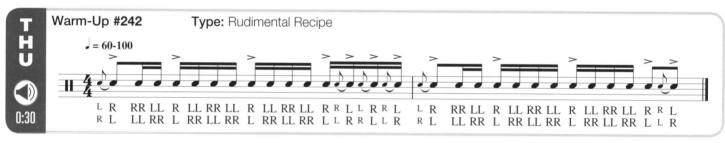

FRI 0:41

Warm-Up #243 **Type:** Triple Stroke

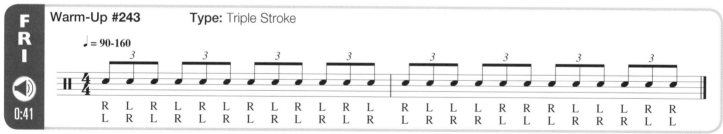

SAT 0:48

Warm-Up #244 **Type:** Weak-Hand Builder

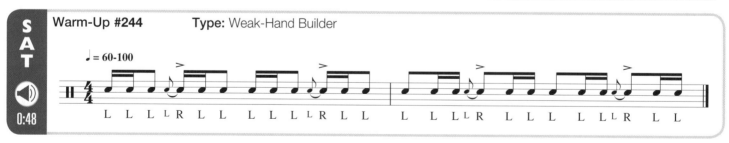

SUN 0:59

Warm-Up #245 **Type:** Rhythm Builder

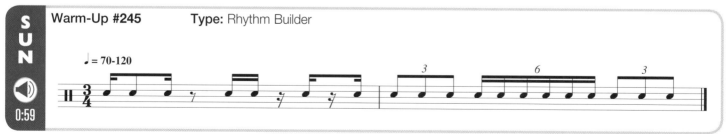

Week 36

MON 0:00

Warm-Up #246   **Type:** Combos

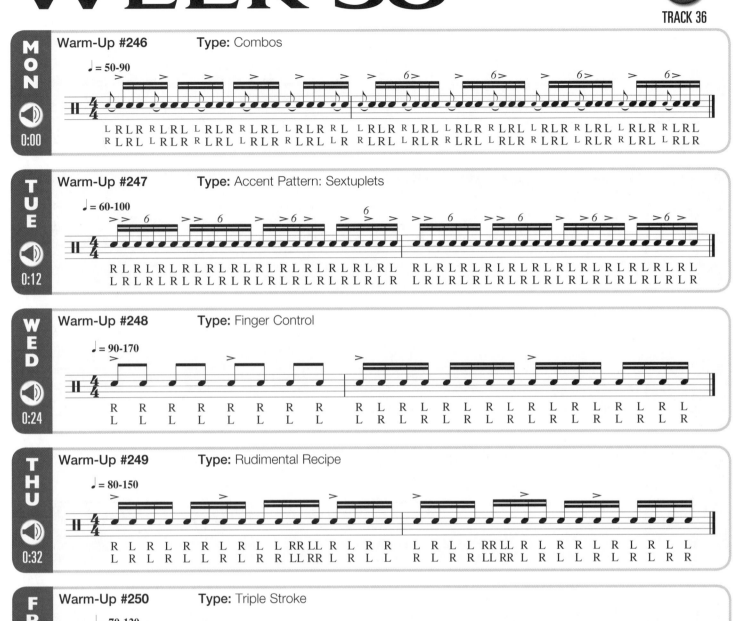

TUE 0:12

Warm-Up #247   **Type:** Accent Pattern: Sextuplets

WED 0:24

Warm-Up #248   **Type:** Finger Control

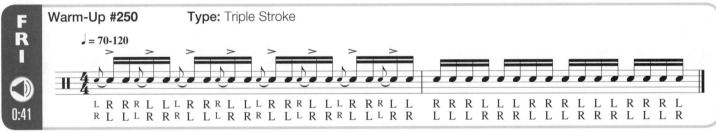

THU 0:32

Warm-Up #249   **Type:** Rudimental Recipe

FRI 0:41

Warm-Up #250   **Type:** Triple Stroke

SAT 0:51

Warm-Up #251   **Type:** Weak-Hand Builder

SUN 1:01

Warm-Up #252   **Type:** Rhythm Builder

WEEK 37

MON 0:00

Warm-Up #253   **Type:** Combos

TUE 0:13

Warm-Up #254   **Type:** Accent Pattern: Sextuplets

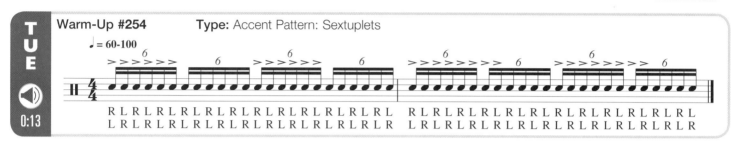

WED 0:24

Warm-Up #255   **Type:** Finger Control

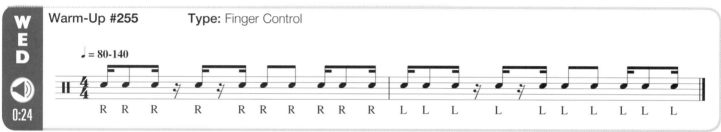

THU 0:32

Warm-Up #256   **Type:** Rudimental Recipe

FRI 0:41

Warm-Up #257   **Type:** Triple Stroke

SAT 0:51

Warm-Up #258   **Type:** Weak-Hand Builder

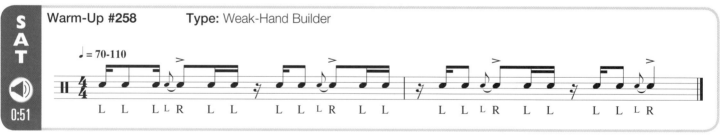

SUN 1:01

Warm-Up #259   **Type:** Rhythm Builder

48

WEEK 38

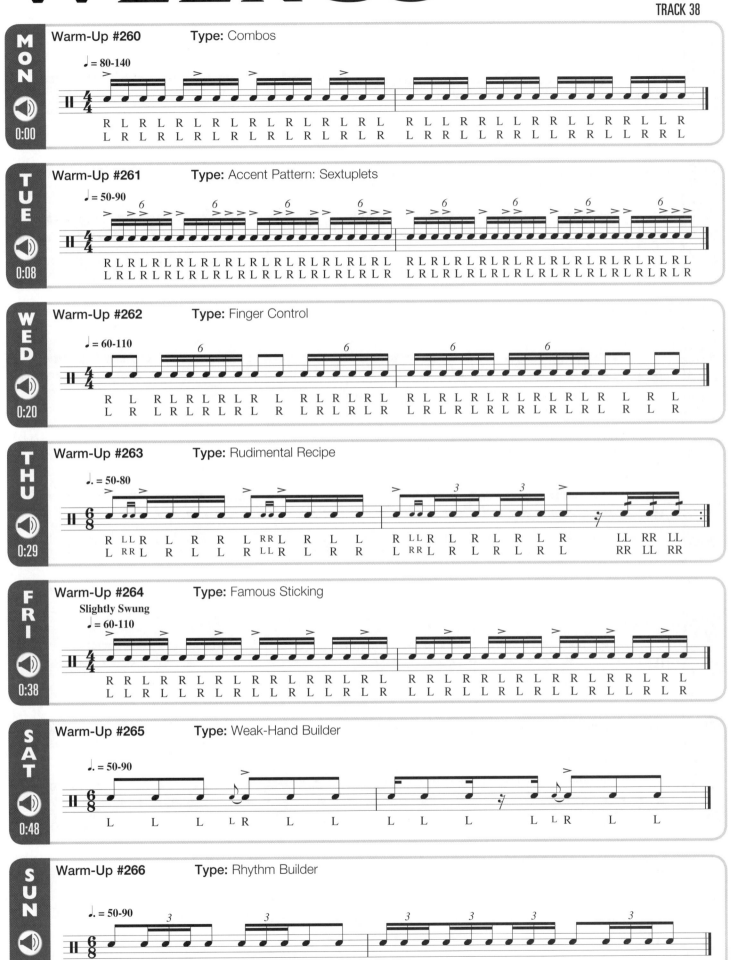

WEEK 39

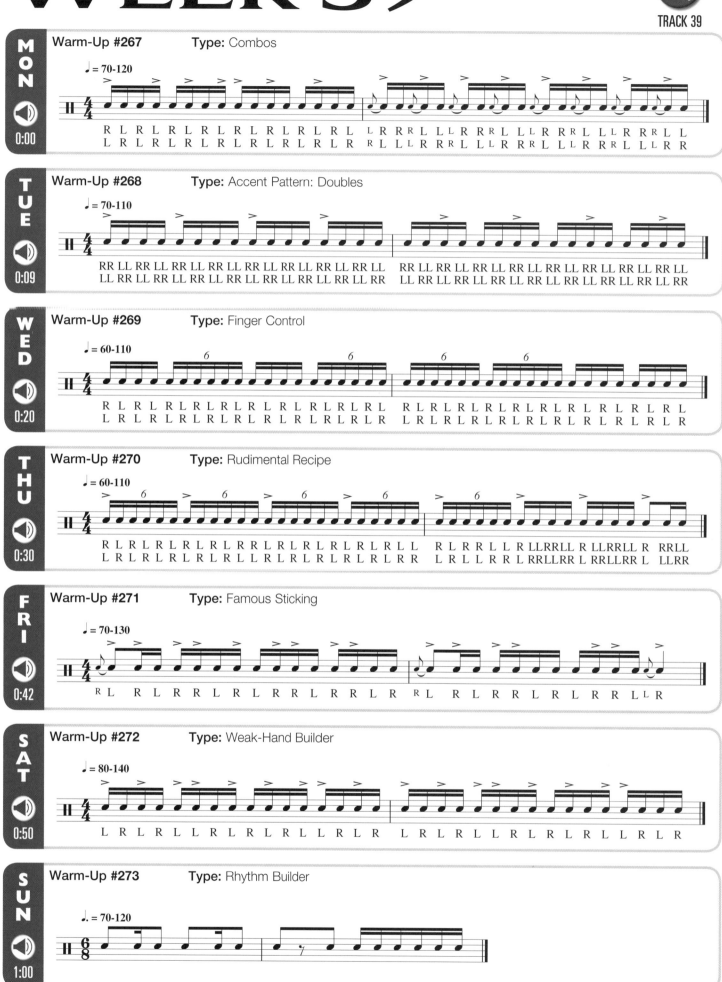

MON 0:00

Warm-Up **#267**   Type: Combos

♩ = 70-120

R L R L R L R L R L R L R L R L   L R R L L L R R L L L R R L L L
L R L R L R L R L R L R L R L R   R L L L R R L L L R R L L L R R

TUE 0:09

Warm-Up **#268**   Type: Accent Pattern: Doubles

♩ = 70-110

RR LL RR LL RR LL RR LL RR LL RR LL RR LL RR LL   RR LL RR LL RR LL RR LL RR LL RR LL RR LL RR LL
LL RR LL RR LL RR LL RR LL RR LL RR LL RR LL RR   LL RR LL RR LL RR LL RR LL RR LL RR LL RR LL RR

WED 0:20

Warm-Up **#269**   Type: Finger Control

♩ = 60-110

R L R L R L R L R L R L R L R L R L   R L R L R L R L R L R L R L R L R L
L R L R L R L R L R L R L R L R L R   L R L R L R L R L R L R L R L R L R

THU 0:30

Warm-Up **#270**   Type: Rudimental Recipe

♩ = 60-110

R L R L R L R L R L R L RR L R L R L R L R L R L RLL   R L RR L L L R LLRRLL R LLRRLL R RRLL
L R L R L R L R L R L RLL R L R L R L R L R L R RR   L R L L R R L RRLLRR L RRLLRR L LLRR

FRI 0:42

Warm-Up **#271**   Type: Famous Sticking

♩ = 70-130

R L   R L R R L R L R L R R L R R L R   R L   R L R R L R L R R L L R

SAT 0:50

Warm-Up **#272**   Type: Weak-Hand Builder

♩ = 80-140

L R L R L R L L R L R L R L R L L R L R   L R L R L R L L R L R L R L R L L R L R

SUN 1:00

Warm-Up **#273**   Type: Rhythm Builder

♩. = 70-120

6/8

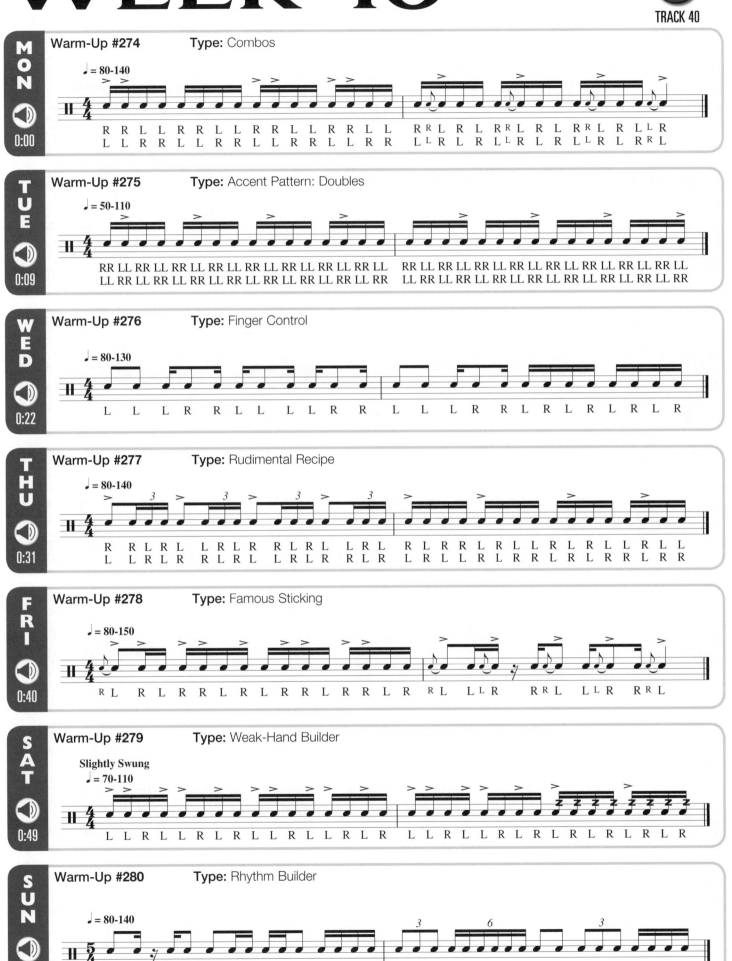

Week 41

MON — 0:00

Warm-Up #281   **Type:** Combos

♩ = 60-100

R L R L R L R L R L R L R L R L R L R L L R L R L R R L   R L R L R L R L R L R L R L R L R L R L L R L L R
L R L R L R L R L R L R L R L R R L R L R L R L L R   L R L R L R L R L R L R L R L R L R L R R L R L R R L

TUE — 0:11

Warm-Up #282   **Type:** Accent Pattern: Doubles

♩ = 50-100

RR LL RR LL RR LL RR LL RR LL RR LL RR LL RR LL   RR LL RR LL RR LL RR LL RR LL RR LL RR LL RR LL
LL RR LL RR LL RR LL RR LL RR LL RR LL RR LL RR   LL RR LL RR LL RR LL RR LL RR LL RR LL RR LL RR

WED — 0:23

Warm-Up #283   **Type:** Finger Control

♩ = 50-90

R L R L R L R L R   L R L R L R L R L   R L R L R   L R L R L R L R L   R L R L R L R L R   L R L R L

THU — 0:34

Warm-Up #284   **Type:** Rudimental Recipe

♩ = 70-110

RR LL RR LL R LL RR L RR LL R L RR LL R L   RR LL RR LL R LL RR L R LL RR L R LL RR LL
LL RR LL RR L RR LL R LL RR L R LL RR L R   LL RR LL RR L RR LL R L RR LL R L RR LL RR

FRI — 0:46

Warm-Up #285   **Type:** Famous Sticking

♩ = 70-120

R L L R R L R L L R R L R L L R R L R   L R L L R R L R L L R R L R L L R R L

SAT — 0:57

Warm-Up #286   **Type:** Weak-Hand Builder

♩ = 90-150

L R L R L R L R L R L R L R L R L R   L R L R L R L R L R L R L R L R L R

SUN — 1:06

Warm-Up #287   **Type:** Rhythm Builder

♩ = 80-140

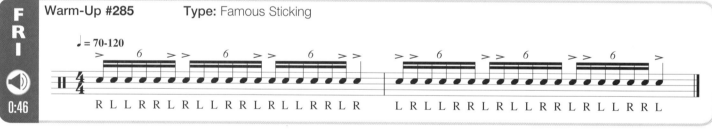

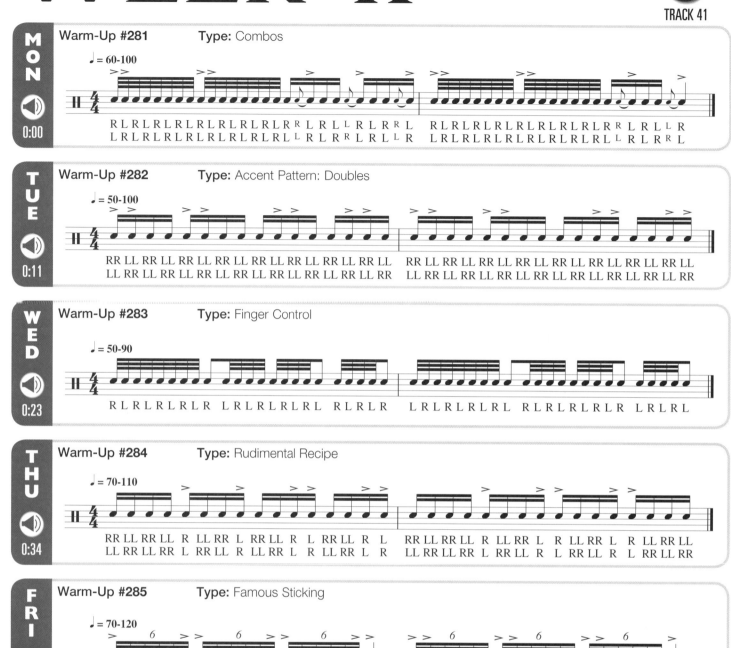
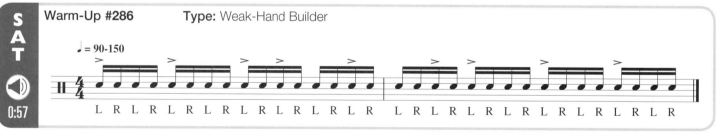

Week 42

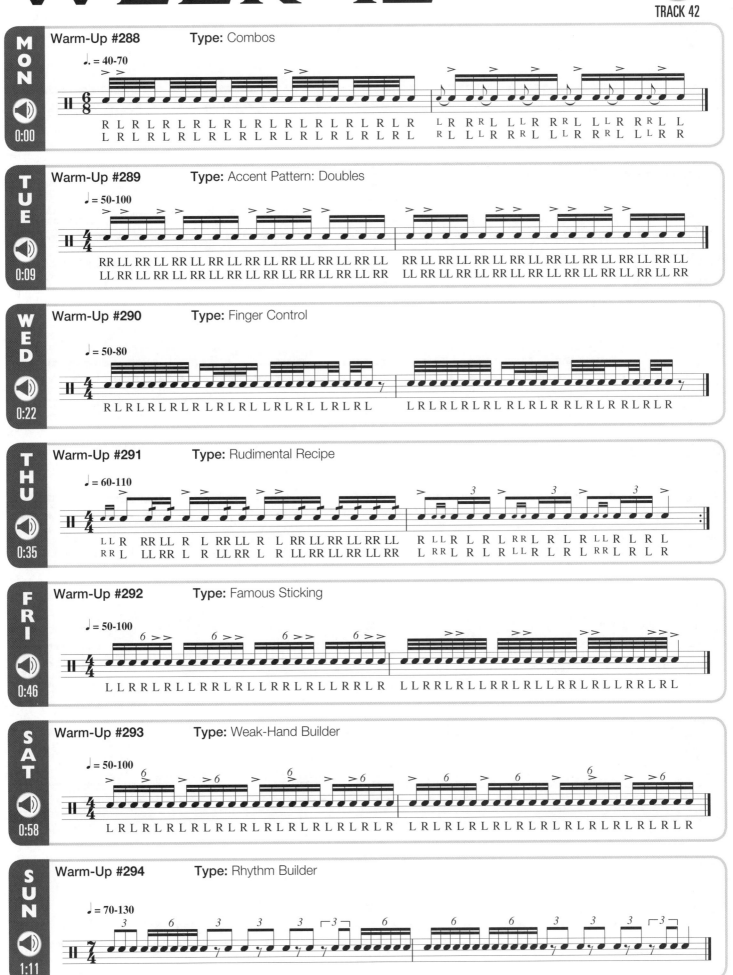

Week 43

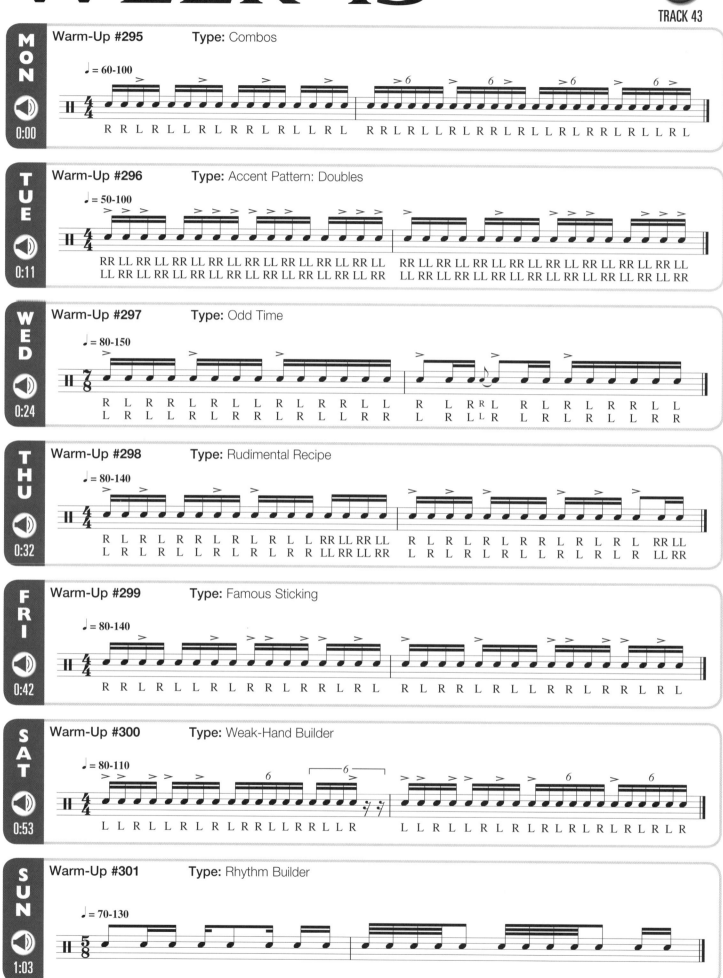

WEEK 44

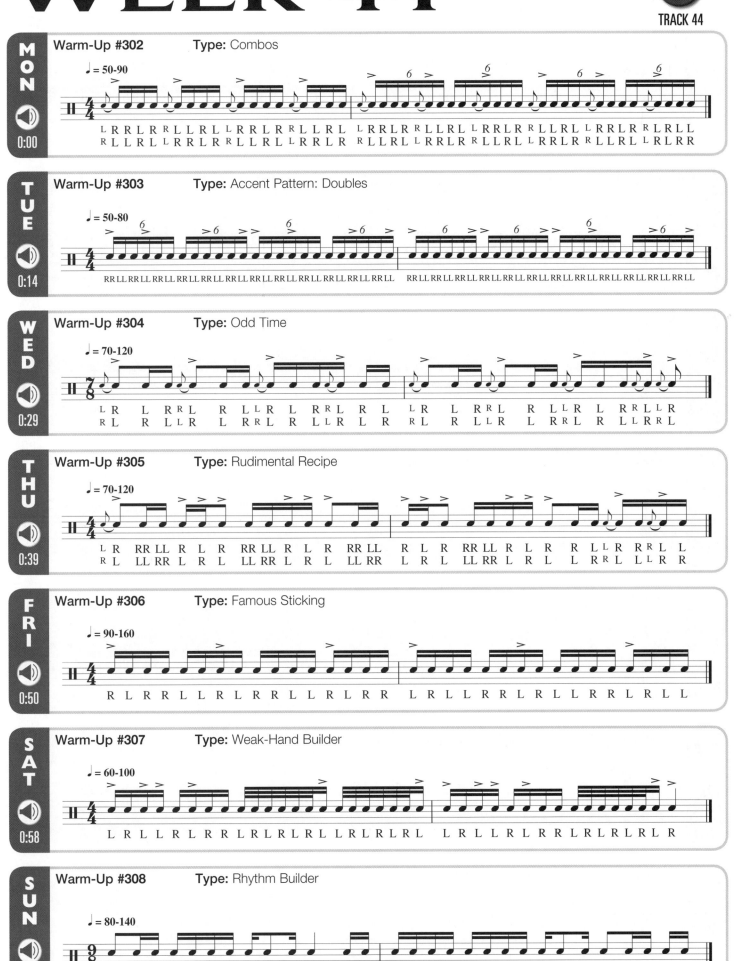

MON 0:00
Warm-Up #302   **Type:** Combos

TUE 0:14
Warm-Up #303   **Type:** Accent Pattern: Doubles

WED 0:29
Warm-Up #304   **Type:** Odd Time

THU 0:39
Warm-Up #305   **Type:** Rudimental Recipe

FRI 0:50
Warm-Up #306   **Type:** Famous Sticking

SAT 0:58
Warm-Up #307   **Type:** Weak-Hand Builder

SUN 1:10
Warm-Up #308   **Type:** Rhythm Builder

Week 45

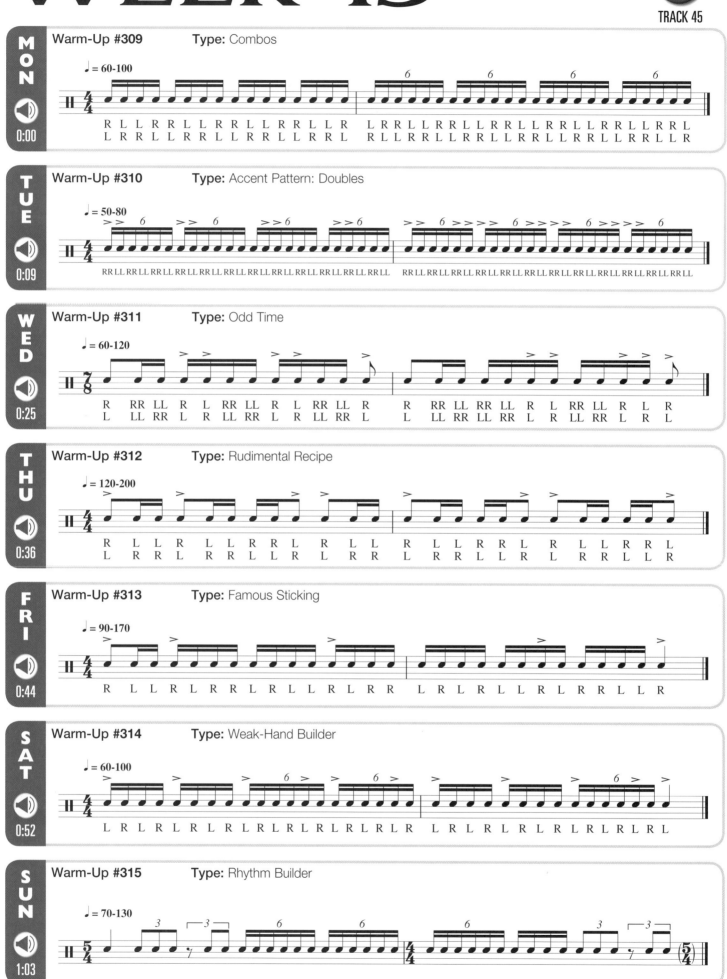

MON 0:00

Warm-Up #309   **Type:** Combos

♩ = 60-100

R L L R L L R L L R L L R L L R   L R R L L R L L R L L R L L R L
L R L L R L L R L L R L L R R L   R L L R L L R L L R L L R L L R

TUE 0:09

Warm-Up #310   **Type:** Accent Pattern: Doubles

♩ = 50-80

RR LL RR LL RR LL RR LL RR LL RR LL RR LL RR LL   RR LL RR LL RR LL RR LL RR LL RR LL RR LL RR LL

WED 0:25

Warm-Up #311   **Type:** Odd Time

♩ = 60-120

R   RR LL R   L   RR LL R   L   RR LL R   R   RR LL RR LL R   L   RR LL R   L   R
L   LL RR L   R   LL RR L   R   LL RR L   L   LL RR LL RR L   R   LL RR L   R   L

THU 0:36

Warm-Up #312   **Type:** Rudimental Recipe

♩ = 120-200

R   L   L   R   L   L   R   R   L   L   R   R   L   R   L   L   R   R   L   R   L   L   R   R   L
L   R   R   L   R   R   L   L   R   R   L   L   R   L   R   R   L   L   R   L   R   R   L   L   R

FRI 0:44

Warm-Up #313   **Type:** Famous Sticking

♩ = 90-170

R L L R L R R L R L L R L R R   L R L R L L R L R R L L R

SAT 0:52

Warm-Up #314   **Type:** Weak-Hand Builder

♩ = 60-100

L R L R L R L R L R L R L R L R L R L R L R   L R L R L R L R L R L R L R L R L R L

SUN 1:03

Warm-Up #315   **Type:** Rhythm Builder

♩ = 70-130

Week 46

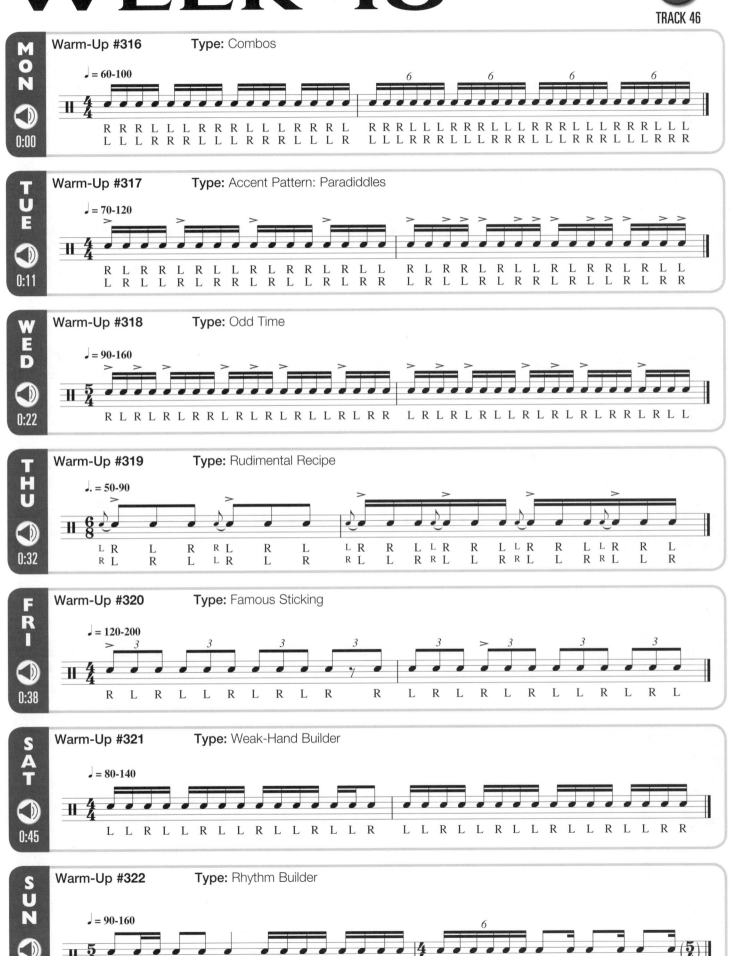

WEEK 47

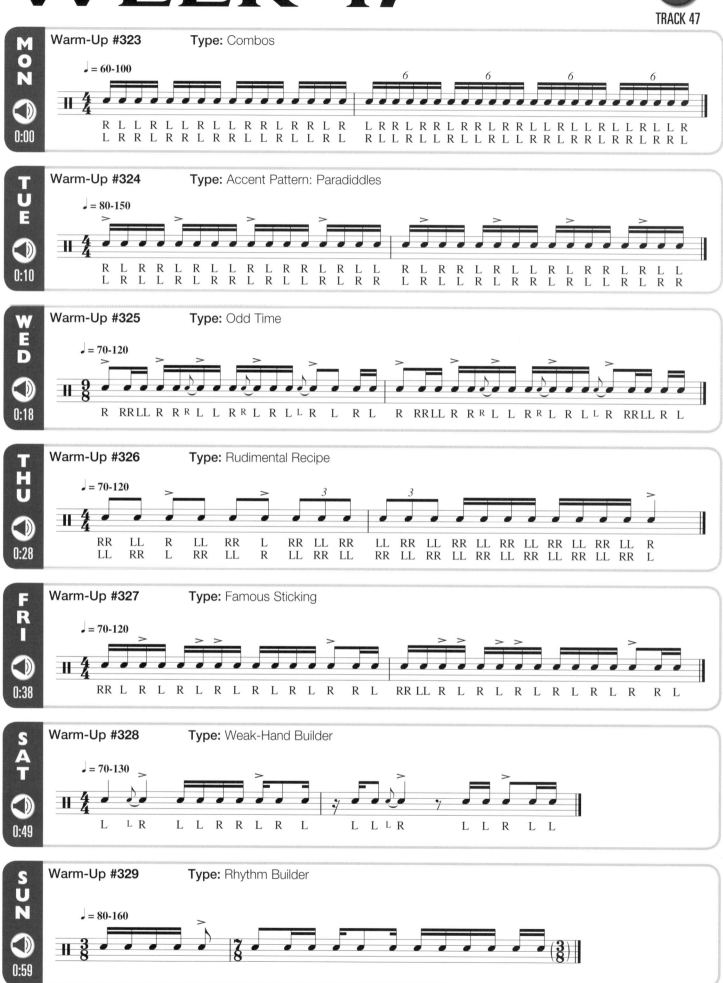

Week 48

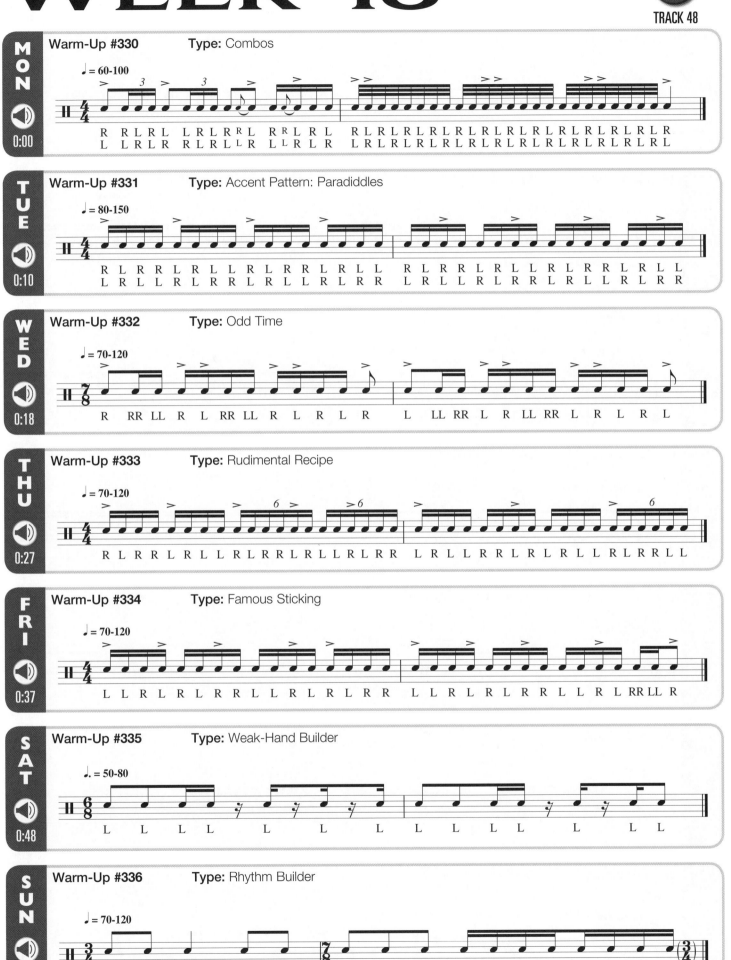

WEEK 49

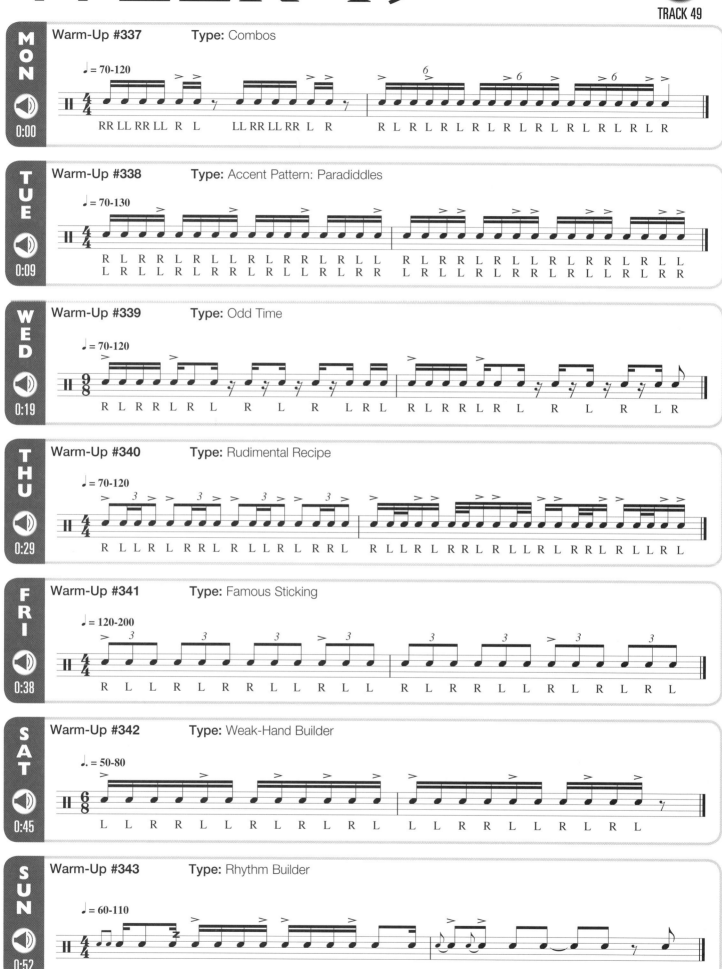

MON 0:00

Warm-Up #337   Type: Combos

TUE 0:09

Warm-Up #338   Type: Accent Pattern: Paradiddles

WED 0:19

Warm-Up #339   Type: Odd Time

THU 0:29

Warm-Up #340   Type: Rudimental Recipe

FRI 0:38

Warm-Up #341   Type: Famous Sticking

SAT 0:45

Warm-Up #342   Type: Weak-Hand Builder

SUN 0:52

Warm-Up #343   Type: Rhythm Builder

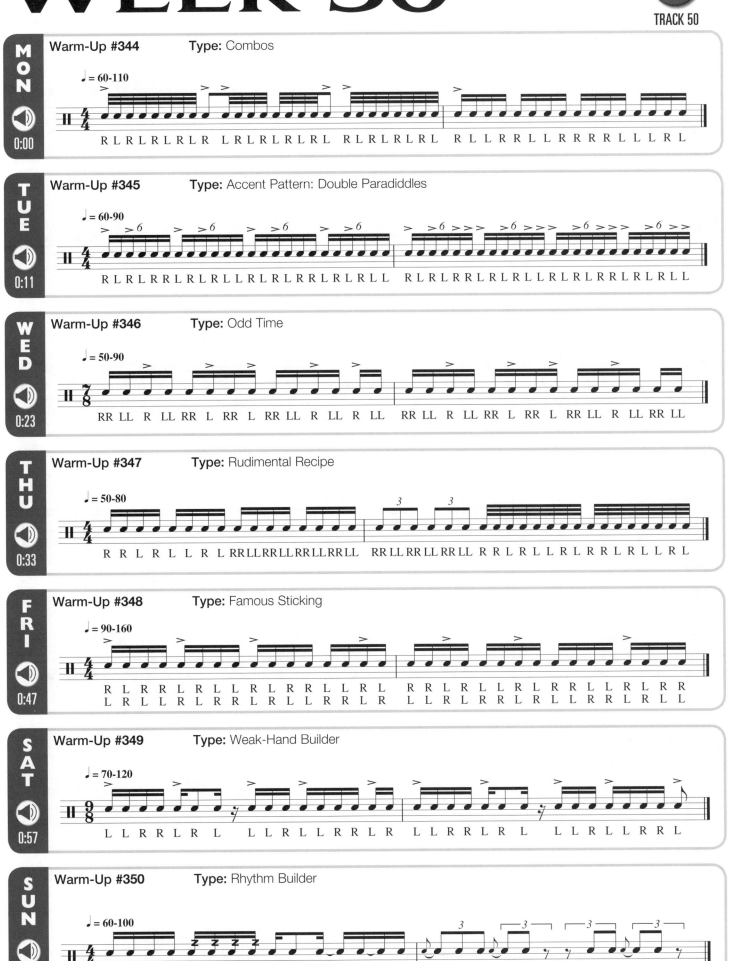

Week 50

Week 51

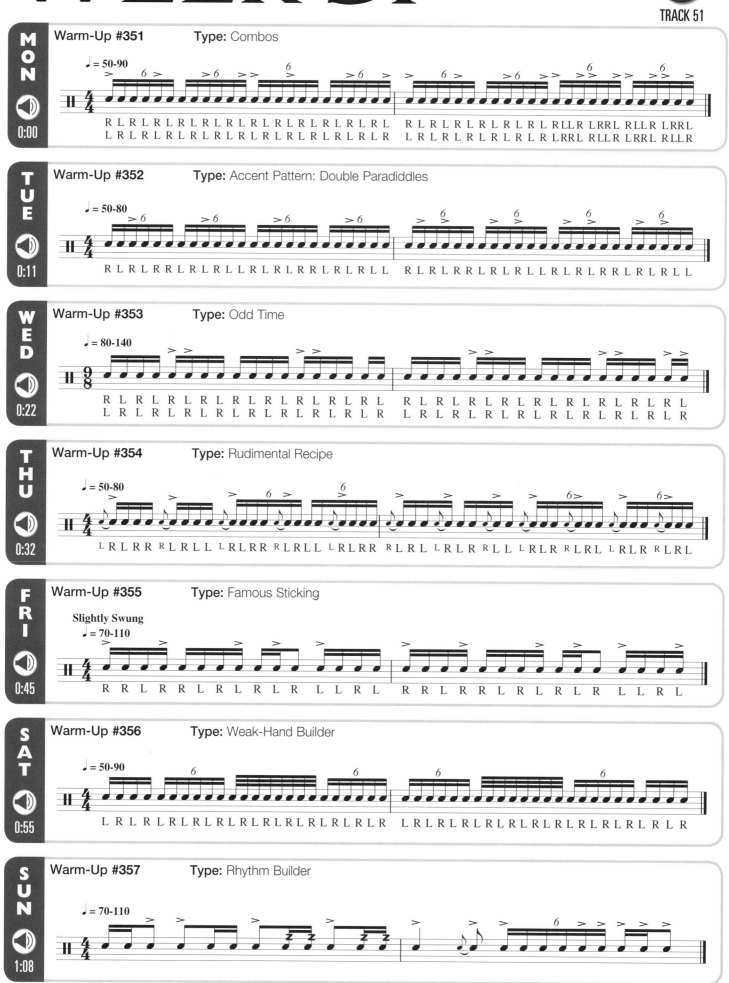

MON 0:00 — Warm-Up #351 — Type: Combos

TUE 0:11 — Warm-Up #352 — Type: Accent Pattern: Double Paradiddles

WED 0:22 — Warm-Up #353 — Type: Odd Time

THU 0:32 — Warm-Up #354 — Type: Rudimental Recipe

FRI 0:45 — Warm-Up #355 — Type: Famous Sticking

SAT 0:55 — Warm-Up #356 — Type: Weak-Hand Builder

SUN 1:08 — Warm-Up #357 — Type: Rhythm Builder

WEEK 52

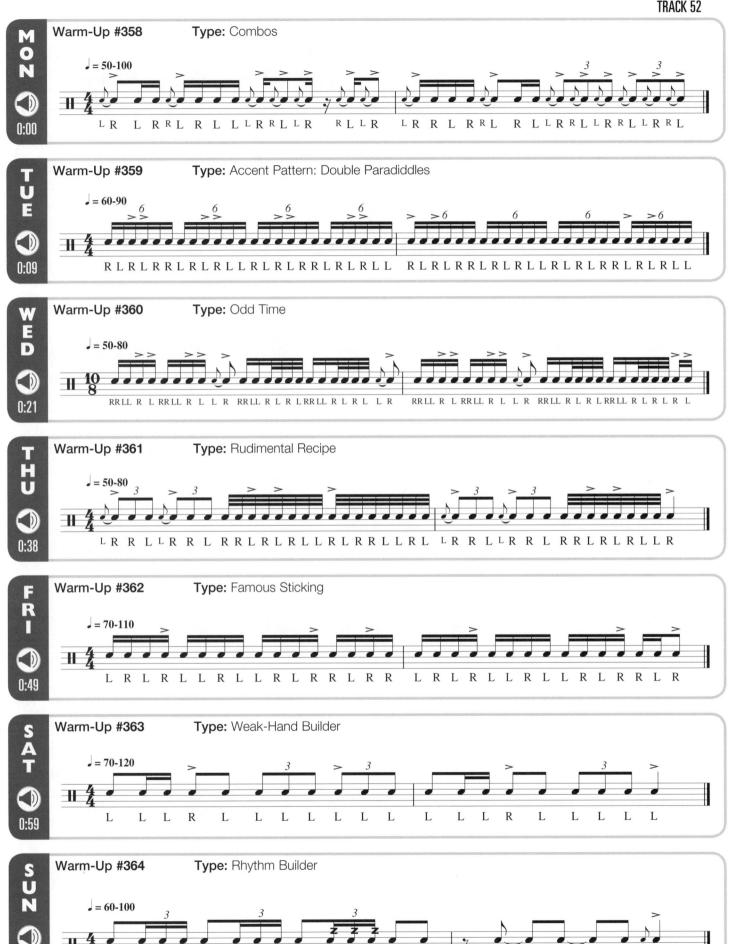

DAY 365

Warm-Up #365   **Type:** Combos

♩ = 50-90

R R R R R R R L L L L L L L L   R L R L R L R L R L R L R L R L R R L R L L R

FOOT OSTINATOS

Track 54

Track 55

Track 56

Track 57

Track 58

Track 59

Track 60

Track 61

Track 62

Track 63

Track 64

Track 65

Track 66

Track 67

Track 68

Track 69

Track 70

Track 71

Track 72

Track 73

BRUSH TECHNIQUE
ACCENT PATTERN

Track 74 One measure of taps with rubber shots and one measure of taps with wire shots.

Track 75 Circle sweeps with accelerated sweeps (two measures).

Track 76 Side sweeps with plops (two measures).

Track 77 Windshield wipers with plops (two measures).

Track 78 Running in place with plops (two measures).

Drum Music Notation Guide

Measures/Staff

Music noteheads are placed on a grouping of five lines called a staff, which is divided into sections called measures or bars. Barlines begin and end measures, while double barlines end the piece. Each staff of music begins with a clef sign. In much percussion music (and in this book), a neutral clef is used.

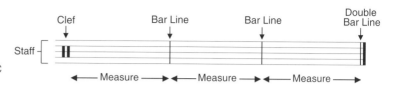

A repeat sign is indicated by two dots before a double barline. This means repeat back to the beginning of the music, or to the beginning of a section marked with two dots after a double barline.

Notes and Rests

In drumset music, notes demonstrate the point at which a stick (or beater) hits a playing surface and how long until the surface is struck again. Rests indicate moments of silence.

4/4 Time Chart

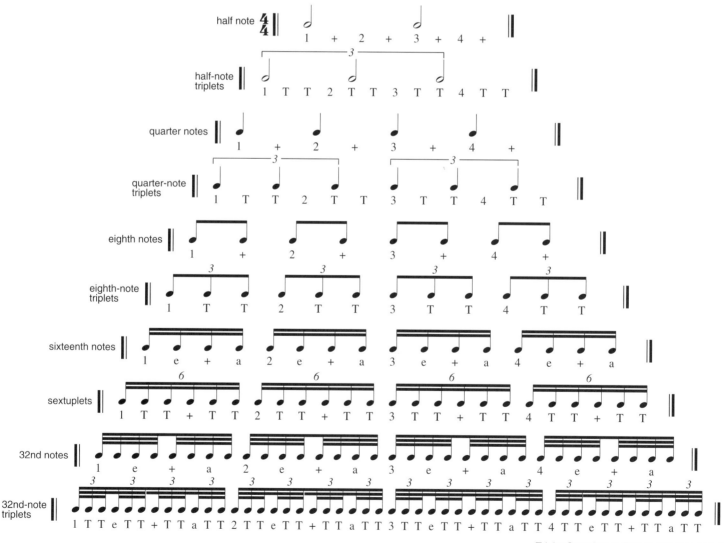

Triplet Counting: "1 T T" is said "one-ta-ta."

THE REST TREE

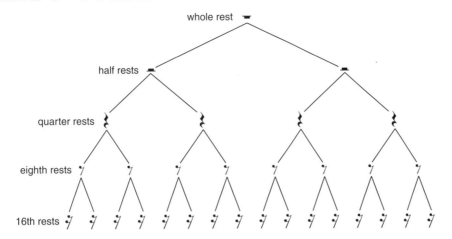

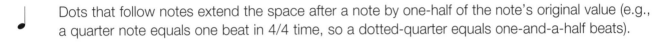

 Dots that follow notes extend the space after a note by one-half of the note's original value (e.g., a quarter note equals one beat in 4/4 time, so a dotted-quarter equals one-and-a-half beats).

When one note is tied to the next, the first note is played and the second note acts like a rest.

TIME SIGNATURES

A time signature is a ratio or fraction that demonstrates how to count music.

4
4

The top number shows how many beats per measure (in this case, four).

The bottom number indicates what type of note gets a beat (in this case, a quarter note gets a beat).

Odd time signatures are used in *Daily Drum Warm-Ups*. For example, 9/8 means that there are 9 beats in a measure and the eighth note gets one beat.

TEMPO

Tempo is the speed of the music and is calculated in beats per minute (BPM). For instance, ♩ = 96 means that you will need to play a musical passage at 96 beats per minute.

A metronome is a handy device that produces a click to demonstrate tempos.

In *Daily Drum Warm-Ups*, a range of tempos is often indicated before each workout. This is a simply a tempo recommendation of where you might want to start and finish.

DYNAMIC/DESCRIPTIVE MARKINGS

An accent tells you to play that specific note louder than the surrounding notes.

A ghosted note tells you to play that note softer than the surrounding notes.

The following shows other descriptive markings used in drumset notation.

DESCRIPTIVE MARKINGS

diddle/double   buzz   flam   ruff
           stroke

DRUMSET NOTATION

Noteheads located on the lines and spaces of the staff designate the drums and cymbals that make up a drumset.

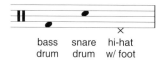

bass   snare   hi-hat
drum   drum   w/ foot

Acknowledgments

I would like to thank: Hal Leonard Corporation, for the honor of writing another book; Tim Downs, for collaboration on the audio; especially my wife, Cindy, for her constant support and understanding; my entire family for their encouragement; Lisa Webb, for her photography; Matthew Self, for his editing help; Don Bothwell, Billy "Stix" Nicks, John Riley, Rob Schuh, Dom Moio, Bart Elliott, Bill Bachman, David Stanoch and my many other great teachers for helping me with the knowledge to be able to write a book such as this; and all of my drum students, for allowing me to learn as I teach. I am also grateful to all of the musicians and educators who have influenced me through the years.

ABOUT THE AUTHOR

Andy Ziker is a 28-year drumming veteran. During a trip to New Orleans at age 13, Andy was so impressed with the rich musical atmosphere of Bourbon Street and a one-man-band street musician playing a set of junk drums that he began taking drum lessons on his first drumset, an old pieced-together Slingerland. When a neighborhood friend wanted to form a heavy metal group, the band Zarcus was born.

Andy played in a number of bands while studying with Billy "Stix" Nicks, a brilliant drum instructor in the South Bend area. His musical momentum flourished with the continuous support of his dad, as he performed diverse musical styles including rock, new wave, blues, jazz, Latin, and pop rock. He improved his music theory and orchestral percussion skills in order to enroll in the music program at Arizona State University (where he studied with Rob Schuh and Dom Moio), and graduated with a degree in music in 1991. Andy also had the thrill of studying with drumming guru Don Bothwell at that time.

Along the way, he developed an interest in teaching drum lessons at Linton Milano Music in Mesa, Arizona. Inspired by his first wife, Rena, he earned a master's degree in Elementary Education in 1995. He continued to play free-lance drum gigs around town, while teaching fourth graders for five years and middle school science for one year. Drum teaching has remained a constant in his life for 27 years.

Photo by Lisa Webb

Studying drumming has led Andy to connect with numerous mentors such as Jeff Hamilton, Colin Bailey, and Dom Famularo. Thanks to funding from the Arizona Commission on the Arts grant program, he has expanded his training to include one week per year in New York City with John Riley.

Andy has published articles in *Drum! Magazine* and *Modern Drummer*, and on the Drummer Cafe and OnlineDrummer websites, and worked as an associate editor for *Drum! Magazine*. He has published five other drum books, including *Drumcraft*, *Daily Drum Warm-Ups*, *Drumset for Preschoolers*, *The Jazz Waltz*, *Play Like Keith Moon*, and a series of e-books, including *Funk Up Your Hi-Hat*, *Funk Up Your Snare*, *Funk Up Your Ride*, *Funk Up Your Toms*, and *Funk Up Your Bass Drum*. He also invented two types of music stands for drummers: Manhasset 53D and Manhasset 53DH. Ziker currently performs with Jed's A Millionaire (LA) and Spun (Bay Area), teaches Skype and in-person lessons at the Rhythm Academy of San Jose, and offers after-school bucket drumming classes to 3- to 10-year-olds in the Bay Area.

Andy endorses TJS Custom Drums and Aquarian Drumheads. For more information about the author and for free video content that accompanies this book and *Drum Aerobics*, go to www.andyziker.com. Andy can also be found on Facebook, Linkedin and Twitter.

YOU CAN'T BEAT OUR DRUM BOOKS!

Bass Drum Control
Best Seller for More Than 50 Years!
by Colin Bailey
This perennial favorite among drummers helps players develop their bass drum technique and increase their flexibility through the mastery of exercises.
06620020 Book/Online Audio $17.99

The Complete Drumset Rudiments
by Peter Magadini
Use your imagination to incorporate these rudimental etudes into new patterns that you can apply to the drumset or tom toms as you develop your hand technique with the Snare Drum Rudiments, your hand and foot technique with the Drumset Rudiments and your polyrhythmic technique with the Polyrhythm Rudiments. Adopt them all into your own creative expressions based on ideas you come up with while practicing.
06620016 Book/CD Pack $14.95

Drum Aerobics
by Andy Ziker
A 52-week, one-exercise-per-day workout program for developing, improving, and maintaining drum technique. Players of all levels – beginners to advanced – will increase their speed, coordination, dexterity and accuracy. The online audio contains all 365 workout licks, plus play-along grooves in styles including rock, blues, jazz, heavy metal, reggae, funk, calypso, bossa nova, march, mambo, New Orleans 2nd Line, and lots more!
06620137 Book/Online Audio $19.99

Drumming the Easy Way!
The Beginner's Guide to Playing Drums
for Students and Teachers
by Tom Hapke
Cherry Lane Music
Now with online audio! This book takes the beginning drummer through the paces – from reading simple exercises to playing great grooves and fills. Each lesson includes a preparatory exercise and a solo. Concepts and rhythms are introduced one at a time, so growth is natural and easy. Features large, clear musical print, intensive treatment of each individual drum figure, solos following each exercise to motivate students, and more!
02500876 Book/Online Audio..$19.99
02500191 Book..$14.99

The Drumset Musician – 2nd Edition
by Rod Morgenstein and Rick Mattingly
Containing hundreds of practical, usable beats and fills, *The Drumset Musician* teaches you how to apply a variety of patterns and grooves to the actual performance of songs. The accompanying online audio includes demos as well as 18 play-along tracks covering a wide range of rock, blues and pop styles, with detailed instructions on how to create exciting, solid drum parts.
00268369 Book/Online Audio..$19.99

Instant Guide to Drum Grooves
The Essential Reference
for the Working Drummer
by Maria Martinez
Become a more versatile drumset player! From traditional Dixieland to cutting-edge hip-hop, *Instant Guide to Drum Grooves* is a handy source featuring 100 patterns that will prepare working drummers for the stylistic variety of modern gigs. The book includes essential beats and grooves in such styles as: jazz, shuffle, country, rock, funk, New Orleans, reggae, calypso, Brazilian and Latin.
06620056 Book/CD Pack $12.99

1001 Drum Grooves
The Complete Resource for Every Drummer
by Steve Mansfield
Cherry Lane Music
This book presents 1,001 drumset beats played in a variety of musical styles, past and present. It's ideal for beginners seeking a well-organized, easy-to-follow encyclopedia of drum grooves, as well as consummate professionals who want to bring their knowledge of various drum styles to new heights. Author Steve Mansfield presents: rock and funk grooves, blues and jazz grooves, ethnic grooves, Afro-Cuban and Caribbean grooves, and much more.
02500337 Book..$14.99

Polyrhythms – The Musician's Guide
by Peter Magadini
edited by Wanda Sykes
Peter Magadini's *Polyrhythms* is acclaimed the world over and has been hailed by *Modern Drummer* magazine as "by far the best book on the subject." Written for instrumentalists and vocalists alike, this book with online audio contains excellent solos and exercises that feature polyrhythmic concepts. Topics covered include: 6 over 4, 5 over 4, 7 over 4, 3 over 4, 11 over 4, and other rhythmic ratios; combining various polyrhythms; polyrhythmic time signatures; and much more. The audio includes demos of the exercises and is accessed online using the unique code in each book.
06620053 Book/Online Audio..$19.99

Joe Porcaro's Drumset Method – Groovin' with Rudiments
Patterns Applied to Rock, Jazz & Latin Drumset
by Joe Porcaro
Master teacher Joe Porcaro presents rudiments at the drumset in this sensational new edition of *Groovin' with Rudiments*. This book is chock full of exciting drum grooves, sticking patterns, fills, polyrhythmic adaptations, odd meters, and fantastic solo ideas in jazz, rock, and Latin feels. The online audio features 99 audio clip examples in many styles to round out this true collection of superb drumming material for every serious drumset performer.
06620129 Book/Online Audio $24.99

66 Drum Solos for the Modern Drummer
Rock • Funk • Blues • Fusion • Jazz
by Tom Hapke
Cherry Lane Music
66 Drum Solos for the Modern Drummer presents drum solos in all styles of music in an easy-to-read format. These solos are designed to help improve your technique, independence, improvisational skills, and reading ability on the drums and at the same time provide you with some cool licks that you can use right away in your own playing.
02500319 Book/Online Audio...$17.99

HAL•LEONARD®
www.halleonard.com

Prices, contents, and availability subject to change without notice.